A Mansion's Memories

A Mansion's Memories

Mary Chapman Mathews

The University of Alabama Press
Tuscaloosa

The University of Alabama Press
Tuscaloosa, Alabama 35487-0380

Manufactured in the United States of America

Library of Congress Cataloging-in-Publication Data

Mathews, Mary Chapman.
A mansion's memories / Mary Chapman Mathews.
p. cm.
ISBN-13: 978-0-8173-1535-1 (cloth : alk. paper)
ISBN-10: 0-8173-1535-7 (alk. paper)
1. University of Alabama—History. 2. University of Alabama—Buildings—History. 3. College presidents—Alabama. I. Title.
LD73.M38 2006
378.761'84—dc22
2006006859

∞ The paper on which this book is printed meets the minimum requirements of American National Standard for Information Sciences-Permanence of Paper for Printed Library Materials, ANSI Z39.48–1984.

Designer: David Alcorn, Alcorn Publication Design

Typeface: Bauer Bodon

Contents

Acknowledgments

The first edition of *A Mansion's Memories* was completed in 1980. The publisher of that edition, Strode Publishers, Inc., later had a fire that destroyed its building, so a second printing was never done.

In the summer of 2004, University of Alabama president Robert E. Witt and Anne Witt hosted a splendid reunion of former University presidents and their families and descendants. The goal was to collect stories and artifacts that would enhance and personalize the President's Mansion. At Anne's urging, I began to think about a new edition of the book to update additional renovations and to add the presidents since 1980. The Witts wanted the book to be available by the 175th anniversary of the University. They gave me the courage to proceed.

The new edition is a celebratory one for the anniversary. I continue to use the house as narrator to relate additional work that has taken place. Not often do authors have the benefit of twenty-five years of hindsight, and I consider myself fortunate in that regard now.

Approximately one-quarter of a million visitors toured the University of Alabama's historic President's Mansion during the decade that we lived there. Many were curious schoolchildren with more questions than anyone could ever answer. In an attempt to appeal to young people and, at the same time, to document the house's architectural changes, I intentionally employed an informal format with the house as the narrator.

I will always be grateful to the people who helped me with the original edition. Principal among them were Frances Denny, Sara Lee Jones, Melissa Hurt, Jim Montgomery, Tommye Rose, Marie Bristol, Sarah Healy Fenton, Frances Smith, John Forney, Jeff Bennett, Jeff Coleman, Jerry Oldshue, Robert Mellown, Jane Paty Waldrop, and Fred Maxwell. Many of these people are no longer with us, and without their support their stories would have been lost.

Joyce Lamont, then curator of the William Stanley Hoole Special Collections Library at the University of Alabama, and her staff were knowledgeable and patient in helping me find materials. For the history of the state and the University of Alabama, I drew on the University presidents' files, trustee minutes, maintenance records, diaries, newspapers, and scrapbooks. James B. Sellers's *History of the University of Alabama, 1818–1902* and A. B. Moore's *History of Alabama* served as excellent reference books.

For this edition I wished for a modern-day University history and hope a scholar is out there somewhere working on a comprehensive history of the University of Alabama that begins in 1902, the date Dr. Sellers ended his published history. Newer books, such as *Alabama: The History of a Deep South State*, by William Warren Rogers, Robert David Ward, Leah Rawls Atkins, and Wayne Flynt; *Opening Doors: Perspectives on Race Relations in Contemporary America*, edited by Harry J. Knopke, Robert J. Norrell, and Ronald W. Rogers; and *Love and Duty: Amelia and Josiah Gorgas and Their Family* by Sarah Woolfolk Wiggins were extremely helpful in preparing this edition.

Professor Margaret Searcy, in a writing class I had with her, suggested the house as the narrator. Sarah Wiggins, Jim Boone, Bob Halli, and Charles Summersell provided expert editing advice for the first edition. Blanche Gunter helped verify some dates and details, and Linda Hyche carefully typed the first manuscript.

For this edition, I have additional people to thank for their stories: Marly and Joab Thomas, MarLa and Roger Sayers, Donna and Andrew Sorensen, Barry Mason, Anne Witt, and Robert Witt. What a rewarding experience it was to talk to them! Robert Mellown directed me to new scholarship about the President's Mansion since 1980, particularly correspondence with Harvie Jones concerning the balustrade reconstruction.

Talented Chip Cooper, with his handsome photographs and his thirty years of experience with the University's photo archives, made all the difference in my ability to do this project. The exquisite new color photographs in the insert demonstrate his artistic abilities.

Jean O'Connor-Snyder and Sandee Gibson Kirby were particularly gracious in their interest and support. John and Gloria Blackburn, Jack Warner, Kellee Reinhart, Jessica James, John Caddell, Preston Clayton, Charles Hilburn, Jim Montgomery, Joffre Whisenton, Lynn Jones, Anne Coleman, Dan Wolfe, Hugh Kilpatrick, Tim Harrison, Donna Maples, Cleo Thomas, Rufus Bealle, Al Willingham, "Butch" Grimes, Jessica Medeiros Garrison, Camille Elebash, and Dianne Golson all kindly provided information.

Daughter Lucy, as a teenager, compiled photographs of the President's Mansion and researched their dates. As an adult, she advised on new ways to organize the material for this edition.

The director of the University of Alabama Press served as acquisitions editor for this project and provided superb advice. I enjoyed working with every person associated with the UA Press. Lou Pitschmann, dean of the University Libraries, and Clark Center, curator of the W. S. Hoole Special Collections Library, were always kind. Merrily Harris was a gem in locating information and photographs, and Stephen Gillis assisted her.

First and foremost with support then and now is my family. A small band of four when we lived in Tuscaloosa, we are now twelve strong. To them—David, Lee Ann and Roland, Lucy and Kip, Catherine, Will, Ann, Sara, Thomas, and Emily—I dedicate the new edition. I hope that these pages will prompt others not only to continue research about the history of the University of Alabama but also to preserve and protect the lovely house that inspired this book.

Furniture from the state capitol, such as the legislative desk shown, was used in a room for the trustees.

Lucy Mathews

1

Building a New House for a Young University, 1837–1855

Basil Manly, 1837–1855

At last the workmen are gone. After two years of construction and more than $26,000 of state funds, University of Alabama trustees now call me the President's Mansion. Hoping not to sound like a braggart, I must confess I like my looks. The trustees wanted me to be impressive, a home to attract leaders to the Alabama frontier.

Small red bricks handmade in Tuscaloosa form my exterior. Cream-colored plaster covers the brick on my front. White lines drawn in the plaster make me look as if I am made of big blocks, but those who glance at my sides see red bricks exposed there.

I do wish my six Ionic columns were marble. They are made of wedge-shaped bricks covered with plaster. Even though I show a strong Roman influence, newspapers in the state are praising my three-story, Greek Revival appearance. I am surprised that no newspaper mentions Michael Barry; he was paid $120 a month by the state for his services as architect and superintendent.

A wooden balustrade on the roofline gives my exterior a balanced front and hides my tin roof. Handsome cast and wrought ironwork edges my third-floor balcony. I really am quite pleased.

Behind me are four sturdy outbuildings. Two will be used for slaves. The one closest to me is the kitchen and washroom. The fourth is a smokehouse, bathing room, and well house. The outbuildings match me in character and are much finer than the simple wooden buildings usually constructed.

Across the street from me are beautifully proportioned University buildings, planned by state architect William Nichols. The Rotunda is in the center of the campus with a row of halls on either side: Franklin and Washington on the left and Jefferson and Madison on the right. Behind them are the Lyceum, Steward's Hall, and faculty homes.

The Reverend Basil Manly and his family are eager for me to be their home. They have been making their own living arrangements during the first four years of his presidency. Mr. Manly, a native of North Carolina, had been the minister of the First Baptist Church in Charleston, South Carolina. He will be my first resident. Board members did not vote until December 1838 to build a residence for the University president. They asked Governor A. P. Bagby, Colonel Aaron Shanon, and Colonel William D. Stone to serve as my building committee. I was not completed in time for the first president, the Reverend Alva Woods, who served the University for six years.

I hope the Manlys will be interested in my yard. The branches and stumps of many apple trees used to build me are lying everywhere. A good cleaning crew would be helpful, and some new trees would be welcomed.

I already appreciate Mr. Manly. Last year he planned my outbuildings, and this year he supervised the finishing touches in my construction. In April 1841, soon after moving in, Mr. Manly gives me a careful inspection. He finds many problems. My roof leaks, and my basement floors, wooden ones the builder substituted for stone, are already rotting because they are so close to the damp ground. I watch the Manlys spend almost $3,000 of their own money for repairs.

Later, on December 10, 1841, I see a letter Mr. Manly writes to the board of trustees telling them that his family doctor says my basement floor is unhealthy. The Manlys have been sick more in the short time they have lived with me than in all their previous years put together. They move their bedroom from the ground floor to the third floor.

Bid Proposal for Construction of President's Mansion, 1839

To Master Builders. Proposals will be received by the undersigned until the tenth day of April next, for materials, brick and stone work, and plastering, of a house for the President of the University, sixty-five feet long by forty-five feet width, three stories high, estimated at 13,256 feet of brick work in the walls and 1504 feet in the columns, 277 yards of slab pavement, 1700 yards of inside, and 750 yards of outside plastering. The brick may be made on the University ground within 300 yards of where the building is to be erected.

The materials are to be of the best quality, and the work must be done in the best manner, according to the plan and specifications, [and] may be seen at the Executive Office.

A. P. Bagby,
Aaron Shanon,
W. D. Stone,
Commissioners

Source: Tuscaloosa Flag of the Union, March 20, 1839, page 3.

Basil Manly, 1837–1855

W. S. Hoole Special Collections Library

From Basil Manly's Diary

Tuesday, April 13, 1841

This day commenced moving to the new building, erected on the grounds south of the Huntsville Road, for the use of the President. It is not yet complete—many things to be done within and without. But rooms enough are done for the accommodation [*sic*] of my family, and it is now convenient to move during the vacation.

Saturday, April 17, 1841

Finished moving; things not yet set to rights however; this will require paving to be done and painting, and a considerable time.

Wednesday, May 4, 1842

This day removed our bedding and furniture. I took possession of a drawing apartment, N.E. corner, third floor. This was under an idea that the health of our family suffered, last fall, from our occupying the basement as a chamber.

Tuesday morning, December 26, 1848

There was a good deal of shooting on the campus last night about 12 o'clock: discharges in rapid succession, and pretty heavy. There were two discharges just after the dawn. There were also two or three discharges Tuesday afternoon. That seemed to be near the Franklin or Washington building. I had expressly charged those who might remain that gunning, for amusement, would not be held disorderly provided it were off the college grounds; but that any use of fire-arms, at any hour, or on the premises would be considered disorder.

Source: W. S. Hoole Special Collections, University of Alabama Libraries.

I delight in watching the handsome students in their dark blue, single-breasted, gilt-buttoned coats and narrow-brimmed hats. I cannot understand why they rebel at wearing them. Students are required to wear uniforms off campus also, but most do not obey. In 1843 they celebrate when the uniform requirement is ended.

As a student watcher, I see the young folks hurry off campus to escape the University's strict rules, and they get into serious trouble in town. They drink too much, steal chickens, and throw rocks. The faculty ledger records other types of misbehavior. A student is reprimanded for pulling his own nose in class, and two students are chastised for defacing a young tree.

As a minister, Mr. Manly is asked to perform many wedding ceremonies. He thinks I am a fine place for a wedding and keeps accurate records of the marriages. For friends and slaves, he has no fee for performing the ceremonies. For others, he charges from $2 to $100, depending on the family circumstances.

My first wedding unites Margaret Cammer and Richard Furman on April 15, 1841. Miss Cammer is well known in Tuscaloosa's social circles as an accomplished artist and writer. The soft candlelight in the parlor casts interesting shadows across the plasterwork in my ceiling. All the wedding guests notice the beautiful patterns of flowers and leaves constructed by the slaves of Dr. John Drish, a wealthy Tuscaloosa physician.

The campus in 1841, as seen from the President's Mansion. Washington and Franklin halls are on the left; Jefferson and Madison halls are on the right. The Rotunda is in the center, with the Lyceum and faculty homes behind.

W. S. Hoole Special Collections Library

Watercolor painting by Margaret Cammer in 1841 is earliest known image of the President's Mansion.

W. S. Hoole Special Collections Library

Dr. Drish's slaves are highly skilled plasterers, masons, blacksmiths, carpenters, and mechanics. When they are not working on Dr. Drish's handsome home on Fifteenth Street, they are often leased to do contract work for others, a common practice. I am fortunate to be the recipient of the talents of such splendid artisans.

The years pass quickly. In 1844 Mr. Manly and his wife, Sarah, are sad because seven-year-old Boysey, a family slave, died of whooping cough. Mr. Manly is making arrangements for him to be buried on campus in a cemetery usually reserved only for students. Boysey will join another slave, Jack, who died in 1843 and is buried there.

In 1851 my second-floor northeast room is designated as the board of trustees' room. Legislative desks from the old state capitol are refinished for the trustees' use. A large wood case contains the books and papers of these gentlemen. William Pratt, a slave owned by Professor H. S. Pratt and now by his widow, built the case. William is often contracted to the University because of his skills as a carpenter and cabinetmaker.

In 1852 Mr. Manly receives iron railings from J. F. and W. W. Cornell and Company in New York to enclose my second-floor porch and encase my stairway. Then I get a lesson in patience! Being busy with repairs on campus, Reverend Manly does not have time to supervise the ironwork installation until a year later. Putting the railing around my porch is easy, but encasing my stairway is more complicated. The railing will not fit my curved stairs and does not look properly attached. Mr. Manly, being the precise person that he is, ships the stairway ironwork back to the New York firm.

Every morning is a learning session with Mr. Manly. He keeps careful records, and I suspect I am the only one who knows that he has two diaries. One diary is for the public to read his pleasant comments about everyone. The second has people's names in code, and he writes about events and professors he does not like. Mr. Manly hopes that one famous scientist in particular will leave so he will not have to fire him.

The scientist, Frederick Augustus Porter Barnard, nicknamed "Old Fap," is one of our University's most brilliant professors. He teaches mathematics, natural philosophy, and astronomy and introduces a course in organic chemistry, the first at a southern university.

Professor Barnard does not use a textbook and teaches by demonstrations. Because there is no University money for assistants for his experiments, Professor Barnard hires students or Sam, a skilled slave, to help him, and he pays them himself.

Outbuilding used as home for slaves who worked in the President's Mansion.

Lucy Mathews

I hear conflicting reports on Professor Barnard. Students see him as an ordained deacon in the Episcopal Church. His admirers describe him as dashing, charming, and entertaining. President Manly, though, writes in his diary that Professor Barnard has been seen drunk both day and night and concludes, "He will not do." Professor Barnard leaves our faculty in 1854 and goes to the University of Mississippi to teach mathematics and natural philosophy and soon afterward becomes the president there.

Mr. Manly's ledger of personal expenditures is a masterpiece. He lists "bread and milk, furniture, clothing, medicine, books and stationery, postage, horses, fuel and lights, miscellanies, superfluities, charities and wife." I cannot help but smile when he is working on his ledger.

My concerns about my grounds are dismissed. The Manlys want me to be a showplace in every way. Each time Mr. Manly plants an oak tree in my front yard, he writes the date and details in his diary. What a lucky house I am!

For fourteen years the Manlys live with me. Now, in 1855, Mr. Manly resigns to accept a pastorate and return to Charleston, South Carolina. The Manlys are the only residents I have known. How will I adjust to new people?

Stairway railing ordered by President Clayton.

Jim Taylor, *Huntsville News*

2

Surviving the Chaos of War, 1855–1878

Landon C. Garland, 1855–1865

Dr. Landon Cabell Garland is named president. He is a Virginian who has taught English and history here for seven years before becoming president. He already knows Tuscaloosa and the University well.

The Garlands move in with a household of children, so I expect lively events. Dr. Garland and his wife, Louise, obviously both have a sense of humor and history because they named one daughter Rose.

Dr. Garland likes students. In May 1858, he asks Rose to have an ice cream and strawberries party for juniors and seniors. They have a splendid time until freshmen and sophomores crash the party. Students do not seem to respect rules these days.

Faculty, townspeople, and Dr. Garland are concerned about student discipline problems. Dr. Garland decides the University must become a military school to keep order. In 1860 the Alabama General Assembly votes to try his plan.

When students return in September, I watch the campus turn into a military camp with strict rules. Students wear army uniforms and live in tents for a month.

The military training gives order, as intended, but it also prepares students for a war Dr. Garland worries cannot be avoided. In November 1860 news reaches us that Abraham Lincoln has been elected United States president. A few short months later, the Civil War begins. Students begin to leave campus to join the Confederate army.

Now I join Dr. Garland in worrying. Many schools are closing. What will be the University's fate?

In June 1861 Dr. Garland announces that the University will remain open. Boys fourteen years of age and older will be admitted to replace those eighteen and over who have gone to war. Lowering the admission age helps enrollment, but many problems remain.

Getting food and equipment are major tasks. Dr. Garland requires students to bring two hundred pounds of bacon from home to use to feed the students and to trade for other supplies the University needs.

Cloth for uniforms and leather for shoes are harder and harder to find. Sometimes sheets and calico curtains from home are used for lining uniforms. Beef cattle are utilized to provide food and to supply leather for shoes. Dr. Garland tries to keep University equipment in good order by constantly asking Governor Thomas Watts and army officials to replace old furnishings.

Frightening news comes on April 3, 1865. The Union army's General John Croxton is headed to Tuscaloosa. The town and campus are terrified because they have heard that General Croxton has orders to destroy the town's foundries and public buildings and to burn the University.

Townspeople are expecting the young cadets to assist in the guarding of Tuscaloosa, and Dr. Garland initially responds. Mrs. Garland prepares for the worst and asks Dr. Garland to bury the family silver in my backyard. Just after midnight on April 4, Dr. Garland sees General Croxton's large, well-equipped army and knows the cadets are in danger. He sends them back to campus.

Dr. Garland worries for the safety of his family and the students. I ache for him as he tells his wife and daughters to leave campus. Mrs. Garland does not want to go, but he insists. "I have asked the students to pack their knapsacks and march out of town with me," he says. "When the Union army leaves, we can return."

Mrs. Garland and the girls go to the nearby home of Peter Bryce and his wife. They live at the Alabama Insane Hospital, where Dr. Bryce is the superintendent. I wonder not only whether I will ever see them again but also what my fate will be.

By morning the campus is in flames. Recent dry days cause the fires to spread quickly. Across the Huntsville Road from me, our library, one of the best in the South, is burning ferociously. Jefferson, Madison, Franklin, and Washington halls are also burning. This is my saddest day.

Suddenly General Croxton's soldiers burst through my door. I feel scared and helpless. They rush through me, piling the Garlands' handsome mahogany tables and chairs into a heap in the hallway. Then they set fire to the furniture, filling me with dark clouds of smoke.

At this very moment, I see Mrs. Garland hurrying into my driveway. She has walked back alone from the Bryce home to see about the University and me. She looks tiny in her long wool challis dress. I wish I could warn her of the soldiers and the danger she approaches.

Landon C. Garland, 1855–1865

W. S. Hoole Special Collections Library

"Little Round House" built in 1860 for use by students on guard duty.

Office of University Relations

She pauses, takes a deep breath, and comes inside. Walking right up to one of the soldiers, Mrs. Garland demands, "What are you doing?"

"We have orders to burn public buildings here," a soldier replies.

"But this is a private home. Put the fire out!" orders Mrs. Garland.

Surprised by the lady's bravery, the soldiers obey. They help Mrs. Garland put the fire out and then move the singed furniture back into place. The turn of events is unbelievable. Mrs. Garland saved me. From my view of the campus, only a few buildings are left.

Days pass, but confusion remains. All the Garlands are back home with me again. I learn that Dr. Garland took the cadets to Marion, Alabama, to avoid further fighting. When he heard what General Croxton's army did in Tuscaloosa, he dismissed the students. He told them to return to their studies on May 12 at a place he would name later.

The cadets obeyed and went home, but the word to return never came. What came before May 12 was news of General Robert E. Lee's surrender and the war's end.

Every day is difficult. Dr. Garland struggles to reopen the University. Joining me as the only remaining campus buildings are the observatory, Steward's Hall, and the small round guardhouse. Dr. Garland considers letting students live with me during the emergency period following the fall of the Confederate government. He tries to hire a small faculty. His disappointment in the fall of 1865 is heartbreaking. Only one student and two faculty members appear.

With no students, little faculty, and few buildings, University trustees believe they must make a change in administration. They ask Dr. Garland to become both interim president and superintendent and to continue to live here. Dr. Garland accepts this new assignment, beginning in January 1866.

I will always be grateful to the Garlands. She saved me, and he protected me during troubled times. Both will be remembered for their courage in the face of war and for their determination in rebuilding our school.

Short-Term and Acting Presidents, 1866–1870

Dr. Garland's main tasks as interim president and superintendent are to replace burned buildings and to find money. His work goes slowly, and financial problems are great. With such a heavy burden and with disappointment after disappointment, Dr. Garland resigns in late 1866.

The Garlands leave me to go to the University of Mississippi, where Dr. Garland will teach physics and astronomy. He later becomes the first executive of Vanderbilt University. The trustees decide not to fill his post and name J. H. Fitts and Company to guide the financial matters of the University. The first private bank in Alabama, J. H. Fitts and Company is named for lawyer and industrialist James Harris Fitts.

Mr. Fitts becomes chair of the board's finance committee and joins Robert Jemison, Jr., chair of the board, to rebuild the University after the Civil War. Mr. Jemison is well known in Tuscaloosa for his wealth and independent thinking. He made his fortune by operating stage lines to transport passengers and mail, and he voted against secession when he was in the Alabama legislature.

The two men are a good team, and they hire architect Colonel James T. Murfee, former wartime commandant of the University cadets, to assist them. Colonel Murfee had been with President Garland and the University cadets when they retreated to Marion to avoid General Croxton, so he is eager to be a part of the rebuilding effort.

Plans are made to salvage bricks from the ruins of the four burned dormitories. But the building team is forced to order new bricks when it finds there are not enough usable ones. After many delays, a four-story all-purpose building is completed in 1868. This building, with its lovely balconies and ironwork, becomes the center of the new University, providing offices, classrooms, dormitory rooms, and a dining room.

Everyone is happy, but I am especially so. I have been alone for a long time and am hoping for a new president soon. I am still proud of my appearance, but I am beginning to look somewhat shabby without a family.

The times are contentious, and the State of Alabama's government is reorganized in 1867. A new state constitution that abolishes the University board of trustees is written. Members of the state board of education, now called regents, are given authority to run the University and to appoint both the president and the faculty.

I hear a great deal of opposition on campus to the regents system. Such newspapers as the *Montgomery Mail* and Tuscaloosa's *Independent Monitor* are harsh in their criticism.

I am eager to have an established president, but it is not to be. The University is essentially closed from 1865 to 1870. A respected professor on campus, William Wyman, is asked to be president, but he declines. Then the door to the presidency becomes a swinging one. First, the Reverend Arad S. Lakin, a northern Methodist minister, is chosen in August 1868, but he does not stay long after a mob, fueled by

Jefferson Hall in ruins after Union troops burned the campus.
W. S. Hoole Special Collections Library

the Ku Klux Klan, tries to intimidate him. Even though Professor Wyman does not like Mr. Lakin, I hear that he saves the man from the angry crowd by hiding him under his own bed in his faculty home nearby.

Mr. Lakin leaves immediately, and the Reverend R. D. Harper, another northern Methodist preacher, is offered the presidency. He accepts, but he does not stay long, either. Will I ever have someone to live here again?

In April 1869 our University opens again with twenty students and Professor J. DeForest Richards as acting president. Mr. Richards had moved from the north to Wilcox County, Alabama, and serves in the Reconstruction legislature. Resentment is still strong against Northerners in Alabama, however.

Mr. Richards resigns quickly, and the trustees offer the presidency to Yale professor Cyrus Northrop, who declines. N. R. Chambliss, a mathematics professor from Selma, Alabama, is then selected, and he serves for the remainder of the 1868–69 school year. He sees the student body dwindle from twenty students to ten and finally to three at the end of the term. Under these conditions, he resigns also.

William R. Smith, 1870–1871

The regents realize they must act to revive the University. They select William Russell Smith, a noted and respected Alabama resident, as head of our institution.

William Russell Smith had been a member of our University's first class in 1831. He became famous as a lawyer, scholar, judge, state representative, and even poet. The regents have faith that Mr. Smith will change our fortunes. His family has a home in the Newtown section west of Tuscaloosa and is in no hurry to move. Mr. Smith wants to see what develops first.

Unfortunately, Alabamians so dislike the regents that they refuse to send their sons to the University. Only ten students enroll in 1870, and four of those are professors' sons. President Smith, a distinguished Alabamian whose selection was an effort to bridge the gap between the regents and the citizens, decides it is in the University's best interest for him to leave. The door to the presidency continues to swing.

The regents ask Commodore Matthew Fontaine Maury to become president in the summer of 1871. Commodore Maury, a Virginian, is a distinguished hydrographer and astronomer. He presides for a few months and appoints an executive committee of the faculty to recommend a new president. The faculty recommends Nathaniel T. Lupton, and the board of regents confirms the choice.

William R. Smith, 1870–1871

W. S. Hoole Special Collections Library

Nathaniel T. Lupton, 1871–1874

W. S. Hoole Special Collections Library

Nathaniel T. Lupton, 1871–1874

Nathaniel Thomas Lupton comes to us from Southern University in Greensboro, Alabama. The new president has been a chemistry professor in Virginia, Mississippi, and Alabama. He studied in Germany under the famous Robert Wilhelm Bunsen, inventor of the laboratory gas burner that bears his name.

I am delighted to have such a distinguished man and his wife, Virginia, live with me. After months of being vacant, I will be in good hands. Our state is happy with President Lupton, and citizens send their sons to school here again. By November 1871, seventy-five students are enrolled.

The Luptons work hard to clean me; they scrub mildew and dirt from my walls. There is no money for repairs, but I look much better.

Mr. Lupton becomes frustrated when two of his major projects fail. He first seeks to have a proposed new agricultural college combined with our University, following Georgia's example. Congress had provided land grants in 1862 to states wishing to establish mechanical and agricultural colleges. Congress said no money from the land sales could be used to buy or build a college, however. President Lupton's plan to combine the agricultural school with the University is a practical one, but it never materializes.

The second disappointment comes when President Lupton cannot get aid from the federal government to compensate for the University's burning by federal troops in 1865. A college in Tennessee receives funds, but the bill for our school not does pass.

During these trying times in 1873, a wonderful event takes place. The Luptons have a son, Frank, born in one of my bedrooms. I like the excitement and do not mind the baby's occasional loud crying.

That same year the students ask that the school's military system be abolished. President Lupton and the regents are unwilling to end the system, but they decide to allow the cadets to choose whether they will be military or nonmilitary students. As soon as that decision is announced, a nonmilitary student enrolls.

Financial problems continue at the University. I need so much work, but there are still no funds to be spent on me. Finally, after three hard years, President Lupton and his family leave to go to Vanderbilt University, where he will be the chairman of the Chemistry Department.

Carlos G. Smith, 1874–1878

W. S. Hoole Special Collections Library

Carlos G. Smith, 1874–1878

The regents search for good leadership for the campus. The presidency is offered in succession to noted educator Henry Tutwiler of Green Springs, Alabama, and University professor General W. H. Forney, but they both decline. Then, in April 1874, the regents and I are thrilled when Dr. Carlos Greene Smith accepts the position.

Dr. Smith, a Virginian, is sixty-one years old. He married Martha Ashe, and his good friend, Henry Tutwiler, married her sister, Julia. Martha and Julia are well versed on the history of our University because they are daughters of the University's first steward. Dr. Smith and Professor Tutwiler have been friends for a long time, and I hope that relationship helps the University. Although he is a physician, Dr. Smith has spent most of his life as a teacher and a school leader.

Professor Tutwiler reads the *Huntsville Democrat* to Dr. Smith. They smile because the newspaper is complimentary of Dr. Smith and says he is an expert at public relations. He needs to be because we have only fifty-two students now.

Dr. Smith is so enthusiastic. He travels in his buggy through Alabama and adjoining states to find students. Enrollment grows, and the faculty increases also. Many improvements are made.

Then a great tragedy occurs. Two students get into a serious argument, and when they cannot settle their differences, one of them kills the other.

The regents investigate the incident and find that some students have guns in their dormitory rooms. The regents tell the faculty to be strict in enforcing University rules. The faculty is to dismiss any student found guilty of carrying a concealed weapon, gambling, using bad language, or being drunk.

Even though military requirements are no longer mandatory, most students participate in the military system. Dr. Smith believes the system keeps order, but he is losing his enthusiasm for such a rigid program. He is concerned that the military requirements interfere with the students' academic lives.

In 1876 the Alabama legislature votes that a board of trustees, replacing the board of regents, will govern the University. The trustees will be appointed by the governor and confirmed by the senate. Dr. Smith, in the summer of 1878, finds himself in disagreement with the trustees over financial affairs. The trustees want to specify how money is spent, and Dr. Smith wants leeway in decisions to spend the money where it is most needed. For example, the trustees approve $151.43 for repairs for me. Dr. Smith cashes the entire amount and uses it where he believes the University's needs are greatest. The finance committee says only $44.05 of the money is actually spent on me.

Dr. Smith would never spend money on himself. The trustees understand that, but they want money to be spent exactly as they approve. They do not ask Dr. Smith to continue, and they name General Josiah Gorgas as the president.

Dr. Smith moves his family to Livingston, Alabama, where he will direct a school for girls.

3

Rebuilding the Campus around the President's Home, 1878–1897

Josiah Gorgas, 1878–1879

On July 4, 1878, there is great excitement on campus! A military hero, General Josiah Gorgas, is becoming president of the University. General Gorgas is a Yankee by birth and a member of the United States Army who became a southerner by marriage. He then served as Confederate chief of ordnance during the Civil War. He comes to Alabama from the University of the South at Sewanee, Tennessee.

I am curious about the folks who will live with me. I am embarrassed to admit that I eavesdrop on a conversation between University professors Horace Harding and Eugene Allen Smith. What I hear is interesting.

"General Gorgas was chosen as president because of his background as a soldier," Professor Smith says. "The trustees hope he will be a strong disciplinarian in handling problems on campus," he adds. "I predict General Gorgas will be a firm, warm leader."

"Do you know him? His family?" Professor Harding asks. "How soon will they arrive?"

"We claim the Gorgas family as Alabamians because Mrs. Gorgas is Amelia Gayle, the daughter of former governor John Gayle, and General Gorgas resigned from the United States Army and joined Confederate troops. Their grown son will not move to Alabama. Four daughters, Jessie, Mary, Minnie and Maria, aged seventeen to twenty-two, and another son, Richie, fourteen, will join them here," Professor Smith concludes.

What I overhear is good. I think I will like the Gorgas family.

General Gorgas comes to Tuscaloosa alone in September. His wife remains in Tennessee until December to pack and move the family. Meeting faculty and townspeople keeps the general busy, but he is lonely without his family.

At night the general writes his wife about me, sending her sketches and measurements so she can plan my furnishings. After a month, Willie, the older Gorgas son, brings the younger Richie to join his father. Richie brings what I consider a splendid present, his big dog. Now I have my own watchdog.

I will be as glad as General Gorgas and Richie to see Mrs. Gorgas arrive. The general's health concerns me. He is not well, and I see him often in considerable pain. His sixty years show.

Richie misses his mother and sisters. He goes to Mr. Verner's school and then spends time with our watchdog.

Finally, Mrs. Gorgas and the girls arrive. She is a smart, delightful lady. Often I read over her shoulder as she writes letters to her older son. I see how much she likes university life and me.

Mrs. Gorgas remembers her early years in Tuscaloosa when her father was governor. Her mother died when she was only nine years old. Relatives and friends took the six children into their homes. Amelia went to live with Almira Woods, her mother's closest friend and the wife of University president Alva Woods. She lived with the Woods family for two years before her father remarried and moved all the family to the Mobile area.

In the accounts of her entertaining, Mrs. Gorgas is too modest to admit being a perfect hostess. But she is. Perhaps the kind compliments I hear at luncheons and dinners are not heard by Mrs. Gorgas. Her experiences with her father when he was Alabama's governor and later a United States congressman, her good education, and her interesting times with her husband and children all combine to make her an outstanding lady.

The family and I enjoy reading a February 1879 prediction by the *Montgomery Advertiser* that General Gorgas will become the "most popular president . . . that the University has ever had." The newspaper reports the respect the University's faculty and students express for the general.

The happy forecast makes events later that month even more heartbreaking. General Gorgas has a stroke. He is not paralyzed, but he now has difficulty talking.

Every day Mrs. Gorgas writes to Willie, who is away studying medicine, to tell of the general's progress. She is grateful to Dr. James Searcy, who comes to see the general often. He encourages the general but insists that ample rest is necessary for his complete recovery.

Because of the general's illness, trustees vote to give him a year off from work. Professor Wyman takes over the president's duties, and the Gorgas family continues

Letter from General Gorgas to Mrs. Gorgas, September 30, 1878

Tuscaloosa, Ala. Sept. 30 1878

Dearest--

The latest letter from you is dated last Monday—just a week ago—I hope I shall get some this evening. These irregularities will continue as long as the fever continues, I suppose. We have not heard anything reliable from Chattanooger [sic] *in several days, but expect to hear of a large increase in cases, if not in deaths.—We shall open here the day after tomorrow, but do not expect to have more than 30 present, on account of the interruption of trains, in every direction.—*

If my <u>box</u> has not yet started don't forget a few towels & the <u>glass</u> from my office. I shall sleep in my own room tonight—I measured the hall today. It is 15 feet wide—just the width of your rooms—The parlors are 20 x 22. The lower part of the house is in nice order: but the upper rooms need some repairs and paint. They have put white-wash over the hard finish upstairs. I think I will have them calcimined and the wood work painted. There is plenty of closet room up stairs to each room; and in your room down stairs a very large fixed wardrobe. In the basement the dining room is in good order, and in front of it Jessie's school room exactly where she would like to have it. My opinion is she will have as many little ones as she desires—Dr. Eugene Smith, our nearest neighbor and Prof. Parker and Prof. Vaughan, who has just arrived all have families of children. I don't yet know their ages—then there are residents more or less distant.—I have Columbus at work in the garden to get in turnips and spinach and perhaps later cabbage.—I give you a sketch of the up stairs and my assignment of them, subject to corrections.—A good deal of repairing and fixing up will be needed, tho' the premises would be regarded in fair order.—What shall we do with the immense hall, down stairs.

Can we not detain Sarah until January and let them all come down this way with you, so that they can see our home. I suppose, however, they have their return tickets by another route"—Any news from the Baynes? I feel myself entirely cut off from the outer world.—I sent the paper containing the article about Dr. Elliott's views, to him yesterday. He will be gratified to read it.—Remember me especially to him. He has had trouble enough with me to make me grateful to him. Are there a good many new boys? We ought to hope so.—
I hope Mr. Bennett has sent your money—if not you will have to drop him a line—Col. Jones would write about Charley, but you will have to send him for Ella—

Love to you all—

Affn.
J.G.

Source: W. S. Hoole Special Collections, University of Alabama Libraries.

Josiah Gorgas, 1878–1879

W. S. Hoole Special Collections Library

Steward's Hall, the oldest building on campus, became the Gorgas family's home.
W. S. Hoole Special Collections Library

to live with me. Hoping my wooden floors will not creak too much, I try to cooperate in providing a quiet, restful place for General Gorgas.

Five months pass. The general believes he cannot assume the heavy duties of the presidency again and has no choice but to tell the trustees that he must quit his job. They then ask General Gorgas to become our University's librarian. Mrs. Gorgas will help him, as his health requires. The trustees appoint Mrs. Gorgas to the post of hospital matron.

Now the Gorgas family must leave me, but not our campus. They move into the University's oldest building, Steward's Hall, making it their home. Soon people begin calling it the Gorgas House.

I will miss the Gorgas family and wonder whether people who pass me on Huntsville Road can see the sadness in my face at their departure.

Burwell B. Lewis, 1880–1885

Again, I am empty, wondering who will be selected to head the University. Newspapers are urging the trustees to choose someone from our own state to be president. After hearing the search committee's report, the trustees vote unanimously for the Honorable Burwell Boykin Lewis.

Mr. Lewis becomes the first native Alabamian to be selected University president. He is now serving his second term in the United States Congress. I have especially good feelings toward him because he married Rose Garland, who lived here when her father was University president during the Civil War.

I get quite a surprise at the beginning of President Lewis's term. My wooden balustrade, which has rotted over the forty-year period since I was built, is removed. Now an ornate iron railing is put on my roof to replace it.

The Lewises have seven beautiful daughters: Louise, Bertha, Rose, Caroline, Nan, Elizabeth, and Nellie. They are all excited in 1883 when indoor plumbing is installed. A small crowd gathers to see my new bathtub being brought inside. The "necessary house" in my backyard will no longer be needed. The first telephones are also installed in 1883. They are battery operated and started with a small crank. I am amazed that the telephone bill for the entire campus is $25 for the first year.

The Lewis girls use my telephone to call friends to join them for picnics. People who pass would never guess how many picnics take place on my roof. The young folks hurry up my back steps from the ground to the roof. There they have the best view of the campus and a private place for an outdoor party.

Burwell B. Lewis, 1880–1885

W. S. Hoole Special Collections Library

Shown circa 1912, this building was named for first president, the Reverend Alva Woods, in 1883.

W. S. Hoole Special Collections Library

The Lewis daughters, left to right, front: Nan, Nellie, Bertha; back: Rose, Caroline, Louise, Elizabeth.

Courtesy of James M. Montgomery

While the girls are playing, President Lewis is working. He is determined to improve the University's financial condition. And he succeeds. With the help of the alumni, President Lewis persuades the state legislature to give our school a $50,000 grant. Then the United States Congress, trying to make up for the Civil War losses, appropriates new land grants to us. I see the optimism that is developing.

In 1883, with the new funds, President Lewis and the building committee make plans for construction. Trustees decide they will name the halls as they rebuild the school. The first building, completed fifteen years earlier in 1868, will be called Alva Woods Hall for our school's first president. I wish I had known him, but he served as president from 1831–1837, which was before I was built.

Amid all the good tidings in 1883, President Lewis receives the sad news that General Gorgas has died. Mrs. Gorgas has been assisting him in his post as University librarian and now she will assume that position.

In a year's time two new buildings in front of Woods Hall are almost completed. Trustees vote that these buildings will be called Manly Hall for Basil Manly, our second president, and Clark Hall for Willis G. Clark, a university trustee.

On October 11, 1885, just when the University is sensing a bright future ahead, President Lewis unexpectedly dies. Everyone is shocked because he was only forty-eight years old and healthy until recently. The next morning, a huge crowd meets with the county's lawyer in the courthouse to pass a resolution expressing regret over President Lewis's death. Then, on October 13, funeral ceremonies take place in the chapel on the second floor of Clark Hall. I feel the same overwhelming sadness that is expressed by the multitude of people who file into the chapel. Now what will happen to Mrs. Lewis and the girls?

The trustees again turn to Professor William Wyman to become acting president. Faculty members take over Professor Wyman's classes, saving money so Mrs. Lewis and her daughters can continue to live with me for a time.

The trustees again try to persuade Acting President Wyman to accept the position permanently, but once more he declines. Mrs. Lewis remains with me for a time and then purchases a house in town on Eighth Street and moves. I will miss all the girls and their activities.

Henry D. Clayton, 1886–1889

The trustees select General Henry DeLamar Clayton, a Georgian by birth and a lawyer by training, as the new president. He has become a distinguished Alabamian,

Henry D. Clayton, 1886–1889

W. S. Hoole Special Collections Library

Tennis players in 1888 near Woods Hall

W. S. Hoole Special Collections Library

Campus view, 1888. Left to right in foreground: the observatory, Tuomey Hall, Barnard Hall. Second row: the Gorgas House, Manly Hall, Clark Hall, Garland Hall. In the back: Woods Hall.

W. S. Hoole Special Collections Library

Dr. Eugene Allen Smith, President Garland's son-in law, with his children on campus, 1889.

W. S. Hoole Special Collections Library

Photoengraving of President's Mansion, 1889.

W. S. Hoole Special Collections Library

twice being elected to the state legislature and once serving as a circuit judge. During the Civil War, his bravery and expertise on the battlefield earned him the rank of general.

General Clayton, a large, robust man, takes a great interest in me. He presents a list of expenses to trustees for repairing me and improving my grounds. My front steps concern him, for I still have no railings. He places an order with Warrior Foundry and Iron Works of Tuscaloosa, and they make my railing in thirty days for $100! At last I have a finished look. I wonder, though, how many notice that I have three different kinds of iron railing now.

In 1887 the committee on university property recommends drastic repairs for me. The front gallery of my second floor is sinking three to four inches in the center. The brick arch underneath the floor is weakening. Many long days are spent in taking up my flooring and replacing it and the arch beneath.

General Clayton's family is fun. His wife, Victoria, and five of their nine children live with me. University students like to visit their three sons, Jeff Davis, Junius Pugh, and Lee Johnston, and two daughters, Mary Elliot and Helen Davis. Mrs. Clayton is a mother to our students, with a kind word for everyone.

The trustees give General Clayton more authority than past presidents in hiring and firing people. So events move faster. In July 1888 General Clayton travels to San Francisco, California, by train to the National Education Association meeting. He is the first official of the University to attend a national education meeting.

The postwar building program that began in President Lewis's term continues through General Clayton's. A handsome three-story building named for President Landon Garland is completed in 1888. Garland Hall will be the Museum of Natural History and will provide more dormitory rooms. Two other buildings, finished the same year, are named for outstanding former University professors F. A. P. Barnard, who became president of the College of New York, and Michael Tuomey, who became state geologist.

General Clayton is compiling an outstanding record as our president. His unexpected death on October 13, 1889, comes exactly four years to the day after funeral services for President Lewis.

Christ Episcopal Church in town is chosen for the general's funeral. Our entire student body meets at my steps to escort General Clayton's body to the church. Each cadet wears an armband of black crepe, and each officer drapes his sword in mourning cloth.

Our drum corps, playing music with muffled drums and fifes, marches behind the cadets. Following the drum corps is a long line of black carriages. I will never forget the dignity and sorrow in the faces of the mourners.

For the third time Professor Wyman becomes acting president. Mrs. Clayton will remain with me until June. I am grateful that this lovely lady will have some time before leaving me. Mrs. Clayton then moves to Eufaula, Alabama, to live with older son Henry, and I am empty again.

Richard C. Jones, 1890–1897

In June 1890 trustees select a third Confederate general, Richard Channing Jones, as president. General Jones grew up in Camden, Alabama, and served in the state legislature. He is a popular choice.

Under General Jones, new activities emerge. In 1892 William G. (Bill) Little of Livingston, Alabama, arrives on campus. He brings a pigskin ball, shoes with cleats, and a canvas uniform to teach our students the game of football that he learned while at Phillips Andover.

Our students like the game and immediately organize a football team. As the most experienced player, Bill Little becomes the team captain. Eugene B. Beaumont from the University of Pennsylvania is the coach. Our University's first game is played in Birmingham on November 11, 1892, at Lakeview Park. We win 56-0 over a team made up of students from several Birmingham high schools.

Sports boom on campus. Students have played baseball for more than a decade. Now tennis and track teams are also organized. A college flag of crimson and white is used for sports events, and the colors become official ones for our school.

In 1892 Julia Tutwiler, the energetic, well-educated daughter of Professor Henry Tutwiler, persuades General Jones and the trustees to admit women as students. The trustees vote to allow white women who are at least eighteen years of age to attend school here if they qualify to enter the sophomore class and if suitable housing and security can be offered. Faculty members study the trustees' proposal, and in June 1893 all agree that women should be admitted.

Anna Byrne Adams and Bessie Parker, both from Tuscaloosa, promptly enroll. They live at home because there is no housing on campus for them. At the end of the school year, they gain recognition as honor students and staff members of the *Crimson-White* student newspaper.

The general's wife, Stella, is distressed about my leaking roof and shabby interior. The roof is repaired twice while the Joneses live with me. In 1895 I am delighted when the walls of my ground floor are whitewashed by covering them with a mixture of lime and water. Plastered walls on my second and third floors are calcimined,

Richard C. Jones, 1890–1897

W. S. Hoole Special Collections Library

or painted, with a wash made of clear glue, zinc white, and water. My Allen and Jemison Company bill for whitewash and calcimine is $18.65! Because supplies are expensive, I hope my refurbishing will last a long time.

At the University, General Jones teaches international and constitutional law and is chancellor of the law school as well as being president. One year he serves as president of the Alabama Bar Association. His respect for the law and military discipline is evident in student relationships. He expels one cadet for destroying a book of military guard reports and another for carrying a concealed weapon.

The cadets constantly complain about the strict military system. They fuss also about food in the mess hall and too few electric fans. Newspapers from Tuscaloosa to Mobile investigate our students' protests.

The trustees appoint a committee to study students' complaints against the president and faculty. The committee reports that the cadets' petitions are greatly exaggerated and that there is much public misunderstanding in the matter.

General Jones's seven years in office are rewarding and eventful ones, but he decides to return to Camden to practice law. In 1897 he tells Governor Joseph Johnston he will not be a candidate to continue as president. I will miss the Joneses and hope those who follow will be as kind and as good housekeepers.

Tuscaloosa girls with chemistry professor John M. Francis on campus circa 1889: Among the girls are Alice Searcy Cochrane, Annie Searcy Keller, Bessie Parker, Evie Harris, Alice Wyman, Anne Stillman, and Bessie Minhinnet.

Geological Survey of Alabama

4

Greeting a New Century, 1897–1911

James K. Powers, 1897–1901

The trustees designate as the next president James Knox Powers, a man recognized as one of Alabama's leading educators. He is a native Alabamian, a graduate of the University, and the current president of the State Normal School at Florence, Alabama.

President Powers's training as an educator makes him eager to develop the University. Realizing how important it is for teachers to keep learning, he hopes to establish a six-week summer school for them. He plans and advertises the summer program, but there are no applicants, so he drops the idea.

Julia Tutwiler visits President Powers on behalf of the women students, who are still without housing on campus. She talks President Powers into converting a professor's home into a dormitory for ten young women from Livingston. They and their chaperone, Miss Sallie Avery, move in, do their own cooking and housekeeping, and complete the year by winning four of the six University honors conferred at commencement.

The public has great expectations for this period at the University. Alumni again persuade the legislature to appropriate money, but many long-standing problems remain.

Rather than setting policy, the trustees attempt to direct the school in detail. Students begin asking board members for permission to attend dances or to have fees refunded. Faculty members apply for positions or discuss problems directly with the board. President Powers's authority is undercut. One trustee even says, "Our institution is being almost trusteed to death."

The student problems of President Jones's term carry over to President Powers's tenure. Cadets are still dissatisfied with the military system. They are unhappier with

James K. Powers, 1897–1901

W. S. Hoole Special Collections Library

the civilian named to the post of commandant, James W. West, than with the president. The students believe Commandant West is unfair in his punishment of them for breaking military rules. He punishes some lightly, others severely, for the same violations.

In 1899 I watch Lou Adeline Powers, our president's wife, read a book written by a former University first lady. The book is titled *White and Black under the Old Regime*, and it was written by Victoria Clayton, the widow of General Clayton. Mrs. Clayton writes that she would never have started slavery but that she did not question it at the time.

In 1900 a well-planned rebellion takes place. Students, led by John McQueen, decide to take action to discredit Commandant West. They stretch barbed wire across four flights of steps going up Woods Hall to keep anyone from entering the barracks. Then they buy a huge supply of fireworks. Students assigned to guard duty are locked in their rooms from the outside. They can truthfully say they cannot get out when the trouble starts, and no one can get in to them past the wire.

Then the ruckus begins. The commandant wakes to the deafening popping of firecrackers and rushes to the Woods Hall steps, only to be stopped by the barbed wire. Suddenly he is hit on the head by small pieces of coal being dropped from above. Only when daylight comes does the demonstration stop.

The next morning President Powers and Commandant West place all students under arrest and appoint a military court to make an investigation. But the cadets have signed a petition saying, "We the undersigned do hereby swear on our honor that I [*sic*] will not answer any questions to anybody concerning the hell raising Thursday night and will stick to each other through thick and thin."

Then the students have a big meeting and decide to go on strike. They pledge not to perform any military tasks, but they promise to go to class, to study, and to protect University property. They send President Powers and the faculty a petition listing portions of the military system that particularly bother them.

President Powers meets with the students and plans to expel the troublemakers, but he learns quickly that the entire student body will resign if one cadet is sent home. A committee of faculty members then meets with the cadets, but the faculty members cannot reconcile the controversy either.

At President Powers's request, faculty members and trustees have hearings with Commandant West. He admits mistakes in adding demerits but minimizes the other student complaints. After many more informal meetings, President Powers recommends leniency in dealing with the students.

Buggy riders in front of Clark Hall, circa 1900.

Geological Survey of Alabama

Cadets in 1901 reenacting a scene in which an earlier class staged a student rebellion.

W. S. Hoole Special Collections Library

A short time later, Commandant West and President Powers both resign. President Powers stays with me until June and then returns to Florence, Alabama. He is soon reelected president of the State Normal School there.

William S. Wyman, 1901–1902

Again the trustees turn to the man who has helped them often in our school's most troubled times. Three times he has been acting president. Now, finally, in 1901 Professor William Stokes Wyman accepts the presidency. When he and his wife, Melissa, move in with me in August, he is seventy years old.

President Wyman has been associated with our University for fifty-three years and is widely known and respected. He was graduated from here in 1851 and returned almost immediately to teach Latin and Greek. Then he helped build our library's collection, only to see it destroyed during the Civil War. He stood determinedly by Dr. Garland in trying to rebuild our school. In addition to his teaching duties, Professor Wyman served as acting librarian through most of the 1870s. Under his direction, our first library card catalogue system was started.

President Wyman's first love is teaching, and he tells the trustees emphatically that he will continue to teach while he presides as head of our school.

I know the Wymans will like me. They already have a family tradition of loving beautiful old homes. They have lived since the 1870s in a faculty house on our campus. Before that they lived in Mrs. Wyman's family home, the Dearing House, on Fourteenth Street.

They bring with them lovely parlor furniture bought for the Dearing House in 1840. They unpack President Wyman's fine library, including many rare books on the history of Alabama Indians.

President Wyman's love of linguistics goes beyond the classics. He is an authority on the language of Alabama Indians, particularly the Creeks. He spent much time recording Indian dialects so the Indians could learn to read and write their own languages.

I delight in the elegance the Wymans bring to me. The biggest pleasure, however, comes from the Wymans's three granddaughters, Ellen, Alice, and Evelyn Ashley, who have lived with their grandparents since their mother died.

Alice is already a familiar figure. I have seen her since she was four years old, strolling at dusk with her grandfather Wyman. They walk to town to get a newspaper, with the professor carrying a lantern to light their return.

William S. Wyman, 1901–1902

W. S. Hoole Special Collections Library

President's Mansion, 1900

Geological Survey of Alabama

Melissa Wyman, aunt and chaperone, with Evelyn Ashley, Alice Ashley, Irving Little, Ellen Ashley, and a friend at a picnic on the banks of the Black Warrior River.

Courtesy of Melissa Jack Hurt

President's Mansion, 1910

Geological Survey of Alabama

President Wyman likes to garden and to share his knowledge about plants. On many Sunday afternoons he gathers faculty children to join his granddaughters and him in nature walks to identify flowers. He teaches so clearly that even the youngest child understands him.

I am a busy place with the activities of the three teenage Wyman grandchildren. Houseboat parties on the Black Warrior River, picnics, and canoe trips are planned on my doorsteps. Many teenage parties take place under my roof.

The burden of the presidency is a heavy one, though. As much as President Wyman loves the University and the University faculty and students love him, he resigns after a year to return to teaching. His strong, consistent leadership for more than one-half of a century is an enduring contribution to our institution.

John W. Abercrombie, 1902–1911

Alabama's state superintendent of education, John William Abercrombie, resigns his position to become president of the University, beginning his term in 1902. He is a respected, well-known educator who studied law here and served as state senator before becoming superintendent.

Dr. Abercrombie's first major decision is to recommend abolishing the military system, a problem that has troubled university presidents for more than twenty years. In 1903 the state legislature formally ends the military structure.

The following year, the University opens its first summer school. Former president Powers would be pleased, given his efforts to establish such a program. Dr. Abercrombie intends to train teachers and bridge the gap between the high schools and colleges. He believes that improving teachers' education will raise the quality of Alabama's high schools and that eventually the standards of the University can be raised.

In 1905 Dr. Abercrombie reports to the trustees that I am in poor condition. He asks board members to form a committee to investigate furnishing me. Until now, each president has bought his own furniture.

Two years pass. Once again Dr. Abercrombie broaches the need for repairs. He suggests that the trustees hire an architect, and they choose Frank Lockwood from Montgomery.

Mr. Lockwood goes to work immediately to make exterior and interior changes. He realizes my structure lacks height on the roofline because the balustrade has been removed. But rather than restoring that, he continues the parapet walls in

John W. Abercrombie, 1902–1911

W. S. Hoole Special Collections Library

order to surround my roofline completely. He enlarges my small south porch to a three-story one.

All my outside walls are plastered and painted white for the first time, so now my sides match the front. Alabama marble is added to renovate my front porch.

Drastic changes are made in my interior. All my original pine boards on the second floor are replaced with white oak flooring. Original mantels on my second floor are removed and replaced. I get new plumbing, new electric wiring, and central steam heating. My modern radiators knock and bump and sometimes annoy my guests.

In October Dr. Abercrombie and his wife, Rose, entertain faculty and students to show off my new features. All marvel at my white interior walls and electric chandeliers.

That same year, 1907, Dr. Abercrombie heads a group to organize the Association of Alabama Colleges. The goal is to raise college entrance requirements and make them standard for all schools. By 1908 the organization is formed.

Dr. Abercrombie's leadership to upgrade academic standards is not always popular. Initially, enrollment drops slightly when admission requirements are raised. In 1909 a star football player is ruled ineligible by the faculty because of poor scholastic work. Dr. Abercrombie upholds the professors' decision.

Three yellow brick buildings are completed during Dr. Abercrombie's administration. Comer Hall, named for Governor B. B. Comer, contains the new College of Engineering. Smith Hall, named for state geologist Eugene Allen Smith, becomes home for the state geological service and for the Museum of Natural History. Morgan Hall, named for Alabama's United States senator John Tyler Morgan, houses the College of Arts and Sciences, the College of Education, and an auditorium. The University Supply Store opens.

On June 30, 1911, Dr. Abercrombie makes his annual report to the trustees. He lists the new programs developed under his leadership and mentions the increased endowment, new appropriations, and a growing alumni fund as accomplishments of his administration.

Then he speaks to the board of his relationship with them. He does not believe that the original agreement the board made with him has been kept. He is concerned that he and the board will drift back into unhealthy practices that troubled past presidents. He says the board is beginning to "administer directly important internal details which in all successfully conducted institutions are delegated to the president and faculty." He lists a number of other intrusive practices and closes by saying he has been effective as president and can continue with the full support of the board. That endorsement is not forthcoming, and the next day Dr. Abercrombie resigns.

I will always remember the Abercrombies. In an era when historic houses were neglected or demolished, they initiated my restoration for a new century. They set high standards in whatever they did, be that their refurbishing of me or their leading of the University.

Dr. Abercrombie enters politics and in 1912 is elected an Alabama member at large to the sixty-third United States Congress. He serves two terms.

5

Cementing a Capstone, 1911–1942

George H. Denny, 1911–1936, 1941–1942

On the last day of the year in 1911, George Hutcheson Denny arrives in Tuscaloosa to assume the presidency of the University. Dr. Denny's credentials are impeccable. He comes here after serving as president of Washington and Lee University for ten years. He is a native Virginian who believes in manners and learning.

Dr. Denny and his wife, Janie, and their three children, Frances, Charlotte, and George, move in. Dr. Denny's friends affectionately call him "Mike," and some call his son "Mike" also. I grin, though, because Dr. Denny calls his son "Buster," and Mrs. Denny always calls him "George." Just as Mrs. Denny is explaining that I will not always look as big and as empty as I do now, the children discover a huge angel food cake with a welcoming note, a lovely sign of southern hospitality. My atmosphere seems much cozier to them now.

The Denny family likes me and enjoys every inch inside and out. Another daughter, Margaret, is born while they live with me, and she brings additional pleasure.

Behind me is still a large field with a barn. Mrs. Denny, a splendid horsewoman, keeps her two horses there, along with a cow and some chickens. Later, young Margaret has a pony and rides with Mrs. Denny.

The children enjoy playing here. They ride my dumbwaiter from the ground-floor kitchen to the dining room above. They hide in the trunks in my third-floor closets when they think Dr. Denny is going to scold them.

Dr. Denny is a strong disciplinarian. He particularly objects to the hazing of freshmen and ends that practice on campus. But in 1916 the seniors decide to have "inspection" one more time before they leave. "Inspection" is probably a carryover from military days, and the term is a milder description of the actual event.

On the night of inspection, freshmen are awakened just after midnight and marched to a remote place. The freshmen are told to grab their ankles; then each senior gives a swat with a slat to the bending students. Dr. Denny hears about the incident and promptly expels the entire senior class three weeks before graduation. The seniors who planned the inspection admit their guilt and plead with Dr. Denny to pardon the rest of the class.

After two weeks, Dr. Denny decides to allow all the seniors except the leaders of the hazing to take final exams and graduate. He hopes his action will abolish hazing forever because he believes it is dangerous and inhumane.

That same year the University is designated as a Reserve Officers Training Corps (ROTC) school, soon after Congress passes an act establishing such a system. The following year the United States is engaged in war in Europe, and the ROTC unit becomes the most important part of the school. ROTC students want to abandon classes and drill all day. Dr. Denny will not allow that, but he does agree to shorten classes to forty-five minutes and lengthen drill to two hours in the morning and two hours in the afternoon.

Every male in school is in ROTC, and many professors join in drills. Uniforms ordered from a mail catalogue are of inferior quality. But even with their ill-fitting uniforms, the students are earnest and patriotic.

The University experiences difficult times in 1918 and 1919. The war takes a toll on the male student body population. Dr. Denny is ineligible for military service, but he volunteers to work in Washington, D.C., and becomes a member of the Food Administration staff.

While Dr. Denny is in Washington, Dr. J. H. Doster is left in charge. Dr. Denny writes regularly to give instructions for operating the institution.

During the war, the need for officers and soldiers is acute. The War Department takes charge of almost all colleges in the country, including ours. College students are enlisted in the Students Army Training Corps (SATC) and are regarded as enlisted men who remain in college and attend classes.

Shortly after Armistice Day in 1918, the SATC is disbanded, and Dr. Denny returns to campus. He finds numerous postwar problems. The University income is spent, and the institution has borrowed from its endowment. Dr. Denny begins working immediately to improve the financial situation.

Then the Depression years set in. During this time, just as before and afterward, Dr. Denny is a frugal president. He prides himself on spending the University's money as carefully as he would spend his own. Lights go out on the entire campus at

George H. Denny, 1911–1936, 1941–1942
W. S. Hoole Special Collections Library

eleven o'clock each night, and his own children are the first to complain. The coal-fired furnaces for the campus are stopped at bedtime and started again at sunrise.

Dr. Denny cuts expenses everywhere. Campus grass is cut with reel-type mowers pulled by mules. Dr. Denny decides it is too expensive to feed the mules all year long and sells them. Then he rents mules when grass-cutting time arrives.

Other economy measures hit the faculty. Most take 10 percent salary cuts twice during Dr. Denny's terms. But Dr. Denny pays the faculty in cash while other schools are paying in warrants, and he keeps the University open when many schools are closing.

On Sundays Dr. Denny walks across campus checking on maintenance and observing who is studying or working. One stop he always makes is at the gym to watch Jeff Coleman count money from the previous Saturday's football game. Jeff's interest in sports is apparent to everyone. A college student, he is sports editor for the *Crimson White* campus newspaper, and he serves as the business manager of athletics. He is the perfect person to give an accurate accounting to the penny on how much money is made at each game.

Our president also loves sports and wants to be competitive nationally. He hires Wallace Wade to begin building the University's football program. Dr. Denny, a regular observer at football practice, is a familiar figure in his wire-rimmed glasses and a worn pipe in his mouth, a felt hat on his head, and a coat slung over his shoulders as he stands close to the line of scrimmage. Sometimes players knock him down. Team members develop a superstition that if Dr. Denny is "bowled" over at practice, they will win a bowl game.

During his quarter-of-a-century tenure, Dr. Denny exhibits his personable and thorough nature. He writes thousands of letters to faculty, friends, alumni, and students, underlining words for emphasis and always leaving a special inkblot or two on the page. He greets students and faculty by name, and years after they leave, he still remembers their names and faces.

Dr. Denny receives numerous tributes during his twenty-five years as president. The construction of Denny Chimes is a project of students and alumni to honor him. Denny Stadium is built with football money made from trips to the Rose Bowl, and a portrait of Dr. Denny is presented to the school. He says once with classic good humor, "These honors are nice, but I would rather be an 18-year-old All-American halfback on the University's football team and a candidate for Phi Beta Kappa."

Rumors fly that Dr. Denny plans to retire. Four thousand students hold a mass meeting in my yard to protest, but Dr. Denny decides it is time for him to leave. In April 1936 he asks to be relieved of the presidency due to failing health.

President's Mansion before Denny Chimes, circa 1920s.

Sylvia Keene Smith, W. S. Hoole Special Collections Library

Denny Chimes, completed in 1929, honor Dr. Denny.

W. S. Hoole Special Collections Library

He expresses his great concern for support of Alabama higher education. "I feel this concern, not as a result of the depression, but in seeing a certain lack of conviction regarding the importance of our college," he says.

Dr. Denny's accomplishments are legion. At the beginning of his presidency, the University had approximately five hundred students, four classroom buildings, three dormitories, and one fraternity house. When Dr. Denny leaves, there are approximately five thousand students, sixteen major buildings, twenty-two fraternity houses, thirteen sorority houses, a football stadium, and numerous other buildings. He is proud because no public funds were used in making these improvements. His determination to make the university the "capstone" of Alabama education brings a new nickname, the Capstone.

Dr. Denny at times receives sharp criticism from the faculty for reducing their salaries and from the legislative committee on finance and taxation for using students' fees to add to the University's endowment. No one can deny, however, that this gentleman's record of accomplishment and his long tenure during harsh and trying years are indelibly inscribed in the history of the institution.

Richard C. Foster, 1937–1941

Richard Clarke Foster is named president in 1937. Tuscaloosans are thrilled because his ancestors were Tuscaloosans for generations, seven on his mother's side and four on his father's. His mother's relatives came to Tuscaloosa County within five years after the region's first white settlement.

President Foster was born in Demopolis, Alabama, but moved to Tuscaloosa with his parents when he was a child. He was graduated Phi Beta Kappa from our institution and then went to Harvard Law School. After World War I service, he returned to Tuscaloosa to practice law.

Dr. Denny is designated chancellor to advise President Foster. The Denny family moves back to Virginia, but Dr. Denny visits the campus several times a year. He has a small, sparsely furnished apartment in the Smith Museum, so I do not see him often now.

The trustees decide that I need sprucing up for President Foster. Five months of repairs and renovation take place. Other bathrooms are added to my lone one upstairs. I feel fortunate to receive such care.

President Foster moves in with his sixteen-year-old daughter, Lida. His wife, also named Lida, died a few years earlier. Mrs. Emma Scarborough, President Foster's mother-in-law, serves as hostess for social occasions. President Foster invites faculty members for a holiday party, and I am especially well adorned with Alabama smilax, sprays of holly, mistletoe, and red roses.

Lida entertains her friends also. Her high school sorority conducts its formal initiation in our ground-floor rooms. On one occasion, thirty-five members bring their sleeping bags to spend the night. I like to think of myself as spacious but must admit my ground floor is crowded with a multitude of teenage girls.

President Foster is a modest man who takes much pride in his work. Sports are a favorite avocation, especially playing golf and watching football. I delight in his love of music. His late wife was a talented soprano and taught him to appreciate operatic music.

On New Year's Day 1938, our football team goes to the Rose Bowl in California, tours Warner Brothers Movie Studio, and lunches with celebrities. Humphrey Bogart, a famous movie star, sits by an Alabama visitor and says, "It's a curious thing to me that the names of football coaches are better known than those of college presidents. I know who is coach at Alabama, but I cannot tell you the president's name."

"His name," says his luncheon companion, "is Foster." Then he adds with a smile, "The only reason I happen to know is because I am president of the University of Alabama."

For summer commencement 1941 we host an important houseguest, Hugo Black, a native Alabamian, former United States senator, and now United States Supreme Court justice. He stays upstairs in my northeast bedroom and chides President Foster for carrying his suitcases for him.

During President Foster's term several male students live on my ground floor. They help maintain security and aid President Foster in many projects.

Our president displays leadership regionally and nationally. He serves twice as president of the Southeastern Conference for Athletics and twice as president of the National Association of Separated Universities.

In November 1941 much activity is centered on me. Mrs. Eleanor Roosevelt, the country's First Lady, is coming to speak on campus. She will spend the night with the Fosters. I am excited because I have never had the First Lady stay with me before. Unfortunately, President Foster becomes critically ill, and her trip is cancelled.

Three days later, President Foster dies of Landry's disease, an impairment of the nervous system. At forty-six years of age, he is the third president in the history of the school to die in office.

Richard C. Foster, 1937–1941

W. S. Hoole Special Collections Library

Outbuilding originally used as a kitchen, as it looked in 1935.

W. S. Hoole Special Collections Library

The campus is a somber place. Flag-lowering ceremonies are conducted; more than thirty-five hundred students line my drive all the way to the Amelia Gayle Gorgas Library. Our president's coffin is moved to lie in state there. Denny Chimes toll without stopping for thirty minutes.

Doctors agree that President Foster's life might perhaps have been saved had the local hospital owned an iron lung that would have been available earlier. Students raise money to donate one to the hospital as a memorial to President Foster. As another tribute to him, the Episcopal student center on Thomas Street is named Foster House.

President Foster was respected and loved by many. A strange air of uncertainty hangs over the campus following his untimely death.

Trustees persuade Dr. Denny to give up the chancellorship and to return to the presidency. He agrees and moves in with me again. Mrs. Scarborough and Lida leave President Foster's furniture for Dr. Denny's use. Lida goes to live with her aunt, Kathleen Foster Forney, and Mrs. Scarborough considers moving in with her sister, Anna Harris. Mrs. Denny stays at home in Virginia. Dr. Denny continues to maintain a student boarder in exchange for house chores.

On a warm night in 1942, students, after hearing a pessimistic speaker talk about World War II, file out of Morgan Auditorium and walk toward University Avenue. There a truck loaded with potatoes is stalled in the street. The students immediately see a way to escape their gloomy feelings. They climb aboard the truck and begin throwing potatoes at each other and at pedestrians.

The frenzy builds. Then the group hurries to the women's dorms. The coeds are hanging out the windows and encouraging the young men in what becomes the first panty raid on campus. Dean of Women Agnes Ellen Harris climbs on top of an automobile to talk to the group. She is hit with water from a fire hose, but continues to talk, and the crowd finally disperses.

For a year Dr. Denny remains with me while the trustees search for a new president.

Mildred Warner purchased a pair of Chinese Chippendale mirrors from the Evelyn Walsh McLean estate and donated two valuable salt-glazed English horsemen.

Chip Cooper, Office of University Relations

Rare winter snow at the President's Mansion

Chip Cooper, Office of University Relations

Dramatic new color in the music room

Chip Cooper, Office of University Relations

Mansion in the spring

Chip Cooper, Office of University Relations

Note unsupported stairway and Waterford chandelier

Chip Cooper, Office of University Relations

Front drawing room
Chip Cooper, Office of University Relations

Close-up of drawing room mirror
Chip Cooper, Office of University Relations

Detail of tea set in drawing room

Chip Cooper, Office of University Relations

Residents and descendants of Mansion residents gather for a reunion. Foreground, left to right: *David Mathews, Mary Mathews, MarLa Sayers, Marly Thomas, Joab Thomas, Robert Witt, Anne Witt.*

Chip Cooper, Office of University Relations

First Ladies MarLa Sayers and Marly Thomas

Chip Cooper, Office of University Relations

Landon C. Garland sofa under a portrait of President Garland in downstairs hallway

Chip Cooper, Office of University Relations

Parents, students, and friends attend graduation reception

Chip Cooper, Office of University Relations

Close-up of cherub on urn in front of the Mansion

Chip Cooper, Office of University Relations

Drawing room before the Sayers restoration

Chip Cooper, Office of University Relations

Drawing room after the Sayers restoration

Chip Cooper, Office of University Relations

Spectacular azaleas in bloom on the Mansion lawn
Chip Cooper, Office of University Relations

Antique chairs and mirror in the breakfast room, donated by Frances Summersell

Chip Cooper, Office of University Relations

Exquisite antiques and handsome paintings grace the dining room

Chip Cooper, Office of University Relations

6

Battling for the Conscience of the University, an Angel for the House, 1942–1958

Raymond R. Paty, 1942–1947

The president of Birmingham-Southern College, Raymond Ross Paty, is chosen president of the University in 1942. Dr. Denny will serve as chancellor again. President Paty is a handsome, impressive man with an outstanding record.

Born in Tennessee, President Paty is one of nine children. He earned a law degree from Emory University and a master's degree from Columbia University. After completing his education, he returned to Tennessee to found and serve as principal of Cumberland Mountain School at Crossville. He taught in Tennessee and Georgia before going to Birmingham-Southern.

Now he, his wife, Adelaide, and teenage daughters, Mary and Jane, move in with me. Mary and Jane are close in age, and many think they are twins.

Another daughter, Martha Anne, remains at Birmingham-Southern as a college senior. The move to Tuscaloosa breaks up a family harmony trio known to President Paty as the "Three Little Words." Mary sings alto; Jane, high soprano; and Martha Anne, whatever is left out.

President Paty builds on his outstanding record here, but circumstances are difficult. The United States is struggling with World War II. Our school feels the effect of rationing, fewer male students, and no money for permanent construction or repairs. Even under such handicaps, President Paty moves forward. He promotes research and begins the University Press. An accredited, four-year medical college is established in Birmingham as a branch of the University. Mildred and Herbert Warner donate the former Governor's Mansion in Tuscaloosa to the University for use as a faculty club.

When the first twelve colleges in the country are chosen for a civilian pilot training program, the University is among them. The course of study for all college pilot training is developed here, and the new flying field, named for President Foster, is now used for enlisted army fliers. Sixty pilots are trained in each eight-week period.

The Army ROTC cadets drill on the quadrangle across from me. Even with the heavy air of war all around us, activities continue. In May 1943 we get ready for commencement. Because there is no household help, Mary and Jane each are responsible for cleaning an entire floor.

When parents and graduating seniors arrive, they are overwhelmed with my appearance. The floral arrangements are elaborate and beautiful. The blue and canary colors of the drawing rooms are accentuated with lemon lilies and clusters of blue hydrangeas. In the dining room are exquisite bowls of white magnolias, larkspur, and snapdragons.

On my lawn are lovely tea tables laden with punch and cookies. Only Jane and Mary know that the football players, who live in a dorm behind me, are patiently waiting in the shrubbery for the party's end. When the guests leave, the young men jump from the bushes, eat the remaining cookies, and dash away before anyone can confront them.

Young people like to visit me. My ground-floor back room has a Ping-Pong table and a long bench for spectators. Mary and Jane have many friends who come to play. When the Patys sometimes travel out of town and leave the girls and me in the care of a chaperone, Jane and Mary usually plan a party. Imagine the chaperone's surprise when she finds several dozen teenagers roller-skating on my marble porch!

President Paty is known for anticipating trends and fostering change. In 1943 he advises Alabama's governor, Chauncey Sparks, to endorse equal education for African Americans, noting that integration is working in the military. Governor Sparks takes a different path, though, stating he favors improving separate education and opportunities for African Americans.

We are jubilant when World War II ends, but now new problems confront us. In a year's time, the enrollment jumps from 5,000 to 8,600. President Paty obtains the use of the buildings and equipment at Northington General Hospital from the federal government to meet the needs of an increasing student body. He begins building six permanent dorms.

Other colleges recognize President Paty's superb record and actively recruit him. In 1947 he accepts the position as chancellor for the University System of Georgia.

Raymond R. Paty, 1942–1947

W. S. Hoole Special Collections Library

Dr. Paty, Mary, Mrs. Paty, and Jane

W. S. Hoole Special Collections Library

The Patys move to Atlanta. I will miss this spirited, active family that called me home for five years.

John M. Gallalee, 1948–1953

After President Paty's resignation, the trustees want to name John Morin Gallalee as president. But Governor Chauncey Sparks pleads with them to change their minds. He wants Dr. Gallalee to continue as chairman of the State Building Committee because his reputation brings national recognition to the Sparks administration.

The board then asks Ralph E. Adams, dean of administration, to serve as interim president. He takes office immediately. The board waits a year before asking Dr. Gallalee to take the job again.

Dr. Gallalee is a quiet, serious Virginian with thirty-five years' association with the University. He was first a mechanical engineering professor and then head of that department.

Dr. Gallalee and his wife, Lua, and their daughter, also named Lua, move in with me. Mrs. Gallalee is a gardener with a green thumb and enjoys my yard. Her first additions are handsome rows of red and white azaleas lining the driveway. Then she reworks the circular flower bed in front. She persuades Dr. Gallalee to install an irrigation system in the yard. My grounds are breathtaking in the spring.

Dr. Gallalee wants the entire campus to match the beauty of my yard. One afternoon he observes students pitching horseshoes on the quadrangle. He becomes indignant that they are tearing up the grass and eventually shows them how to replace it.

Our president lost a leg in a train accident while a student at the University of Virginia. He wears an artificial leg, and to accommodate him, an elevator is installed in the space formerly used for my dumbwaiter. He sometimes uses a walking stick but never speaks of his accident. Most of his closest friends do not even know what happened.

A love of learning is a distinguishing trait of Dr. Gallalee. He makes a habit of slipping into classes on campus without warning the professor. He especially likes to attend the outstanding lectures of Dean Lee Bidgood of the College of Commerce and Business Administration.

During a gubernatorial campaign, one of the law professors, Jeff Bennett, visits Dr. Gallalee. Professor Bennett wants to be active in supporting a particular candidate but is concerned that his activities will compromise the University. "Members of our

John M. Gallalee, 1948–1953

W. S. Hoole Special Collections Library

Lua Gallalee Martin tosses her bridal bouquet to attendants Betty Boone, Ellen Martin, and Jeppie Adams Gallalee after the wedding in the Mansion on June 7, 1942. The back screened door opens to a three-story porch with exterior wooden stairs going from the top floor to the ground.

Courtesy of Lua Gallalee Martin

faculty do not resign their citizenship by virtue of their appointment," Dr. Gallalee says. "Work hard for your candidate." But Dr. Gallalee adds with a grin, "My candidate is going to beat your candidate."

The Gallalees bring another lovely wedding to me. On a warm June day, daughter Lua marries Gordon Martin. I am filled with the heavy aroma of magnolias, lilies, and gardenias. Lua, in a lovely white organdy gown, sweeps down my staircase to the ceremony in the second-floor drawing room. A beautiful wedding cake and happy guests await the bride and groom afterward in a reception on the ground floor.

Dr. Gallalee begins a School of Dentistry as part of the Birmingham medical complex. He establishes a School of Nursing, begins the Psychological Services Clinic, and starts an FM radio station. In spite of these new programs, however, enrollment drops surprisingly. Dr. Gallalee attributes the decline to fewer World War II veterans in school, a change in the national birth rate, and more young men enlisting in the Korean conflict. Dr. Gallalee grants leaves of absence to faculty members serving in the military during the Korean War.

Religious aspects of campus life are foremost in Dr. Gallalee's mind. Twenty-seven religious courses are offered, and five churches sponsor student centers on campus.

At seventy years of age in June 1953, Dr. Gallalee announces his retirement. At his last commencement in Foster Auditorium, eight hundred laudatory letters are presented to him from alumni and friends. Dr. Gallalee is touched and then jokingly asks, "Who is going to answer all these letters?" Dr. Gallalee's sense of humor causes him to remark in his final report to the trustees that his last year was free of firecracker wars and panty raids on campus.

The Gallalees have cared well for me, and I regret their leaving. Dr. Gallalee presided with dignity and good humor, and Mrs. Gallalee supervised my first extensive landscaping program.

Oliver C. Carmichael, 1953–1956

After President Gallalee retires, the dean of the College of Commerce and Business Administration, Lee Bidgood, becomes interim president for the summer. I spend the summer alone.

In 1953 Dr. Oliver Cromwell Carmichael and his wife, Mae, join me. The national media laud Dr. Carmichael as one of America's leading educators. He becomes

Dr. Carmichael and Dean Lee Bidgood in Dr. Carmichael's office.
Andy Russell, Office of University Relations

Dr. and Mrs. O. C. Carmichael

W. S. Hoole Special Collections Library

president after seven years as head of the Carnegie Foundation for the Advancement of Teaching.

A native of Goodwater, Alabama, Dr. Carmichael has been a Rhodes scholar, president of the Alabama College for Women, chancellor of Vanderbilt University, and chairman of the board of trustees of New York State University. Now sixty-one years old, he has been awarded sixteen honorary college and university degrees in recognition of his leadership in education. Excited by Dr. Carmichael's leadership and national reputation, the faculty and Tuscaloosa community begin to rethink the potential of the University and its role in higher education.

The trustees decide it is time to purchase appropriate furniture for me. Each resident has furnished me in the past, but few families had the large antique pieces needed for my sixteen-foot ceilings and barn-sized rooms.

Now three Tuscaloosa ladies, Mildred Westervelt Warner, Jeanette Foster Redel, and Ira Brasfield Moody, are asked to select furnishings. The three are good friends and are well known in the community. Mrs. Warner's family owns Gulf States Paper Company, and she is the chief operating officer. She is also an avid antiques collector. Mrs. Redel is also a collector, and Mrs. Moody and her husband purchased the house that Rose Garland Lewis lived in after President Lewis died. I already feel connected to these ladies. They seem to underscore that I am more than a campus building; I am a symbol of excellence in Alabama.

Trustees allocate some money for the committee to use. The Carmichaels are pleased, but I am ecstatic! Since Dr. Abercrombie first asked for furniture for me in 1905, I have been patiently biding my time.

The long years I waited now seem far in the past. Lovely pieces arrive daily. The ladies spend the money for a pair of Chinese Chippendale mirrors, a handsome desk and chest, ornate chairs, mahogany tables, and graceful lamps. Once the money is spent, Mrs. Warner begins giving antiques from her own collection. Oriental rugs, old maps, valuable oil paintings, and delicate porcelains are welcome additions.

For an entire year, the three ladies work feverishly. They replace my drawing-room mantels with ones from Louisiana pine purchased from a planter's home. Mrs. Warner directs the installation of ceiling lighting for the handsome oil paintings that she donated. As finishing touches, the ladies select elegant draperies and popular wall colors. I truly must be one of the most fortunate houses in Alabama!

Mrs. Warner's artistic talents range from antiques to flower arranging. She often brings baskets of brown orchids and other unusual blossoms to decorate for a party. She and Dr. Carmichael disagree amicably over a Houdon bust, a prized possession of Dr. Carmichael's. Mrs. Warner does not like it and moves it out of sight when she helps in arranging for receptions. As soon as Mrs. Warner's back is turned, Dr. Carmichael, in a wink, moves the statue back into prominent view.

The Carmichaels are a reserved, private couple. They like to entertain small groups of friends, and their three grown sons come to visit them periodically.

Mrs. Carmichael is an avid bridge player and belongs to a group known as the Storm Club. The name comes from the practice of never planning when or where the group will meet. One day the ladies get together and simply storm one of the other members by surprise. Mrs. Carmichael is sick the day her turn comes, but she enjoys bridge so much she simply invites the members to come upstairs to her bedroom for a game.

In February 1956 the eyes of the nation focus on us. A young African American woman, Autherine Juanita Lucy, who had applied to attend school here more than three years ago, is finally admitted. She will be the first African American to attend school here.

Dr. Carmichael hopes for an orderly transition. He knew when he accepted the presidency that a court ruling would be made to bar the University from refusing admission to qualified black people on the basis of race. Earlier he had made a speech urging tolerance. "It is difficult," he said, "to legislate and hand down court decrees on folkways and traditions, but with mutual understanding and clear thinking the segregation problem can be worked out just as it has been worked out in the armed services."

The administration underestimates the amount of opposition Autherine Lucy will encounter. All his life, Dr. Carmichael has had enormous respect for the individual, regardless of his or her status or origin. He finds it difficult to believe that anyone would do wrong or show a lack of respect for the University.

No hostility is shown on the first day of classes, and some students express good wishes to Autherine. Then the cross burnings begin. The eight-foot-tall crosses burned in my yard are shocking.

During the first week of the semester, students congregate one night, make a mock cross of old socks, and burn it on University Avenue. Then they march into my driveway to see Dr. Carmichael. Mrs. Carmichael tells them he is away. The jeering crowd chants, "Keep Bama white." I cannot help but think of the black men who helped to build me. Then the mob moves downtown. The faces of the crowd are angry ones. A student climbs the flagpole in the center of town and delivers an impassioned speech against integration.

No one is prepared for the explosion of violence the following night. The crowd mingling on campus is different; this time students are in the minority, and outsiders make up the majority. Another inflammatory speech is made. Walter Flowers, Student Government Association president, tries to calm the crowd.

Abruptly the crowd moves toward my yard again. They demand to see Dr. Carmichael. He comes out on my porch and warns, "Think about what you are doing and do not act in haste." Firecrackers pop, and gravel flies; the mob heckles and boos. Some students are embarrassed about the disrespect shown our president and disperse. But the outsiders are more difficult to manage.

The remainder of the mob now proceeds down University Avenue. A Greyhound bus is rocked severely; gasoline is poured across the street in front of the Student Union Building and then ignited. I feel as frightened and as helpless as I did during the Civil War.

The next morning Autherine begins her worst day. An unfriendly crowd greets her as she attends class. Racial slurs, pushing, and shoving are rampant in the mob. Jeff Bennett, now administrative vice president, and Dean of Women Sarah Healy risk their lives to help the new student escape after class. Bricks, rocks, and eggs are hurled at them as Mr. Bennett drives Autherine and Mrs. Healy through an outspoken throng.

Dr. Carmichael says in a faculty meeting that afternoon, "We are on the brink of disgrace." He sees the issue not as segregation versus integration but as law and order versus anarchy.

A voice of reason during the trouble is *Tuscaloosa News* publisher Buford Boone. On the day following the worst riot, he writes a front-page, Pulitzer Prize–winning editorial titled "What a Price for Peace." His editorial issues a strong indictment of the riots and a plea for law and order. Throughout this difficult period for the University, Mr. Boone urges moderation for blacks and whites.

In an emergency meeting the trustees vote to exclude Autherine Lucy from class until further notice. This, they say, is for her safety and that of other students and faculty. Dr. Carmichael hopes to readmit her when conditions stabilize. But the National Association for the Advancement of Colored People (NAACP) files a suit against the University for contempt of court. The NAACP says that not allowing Autherine to attend class is a cunning strategy to deny her rights. Many accusations are made. At the end of February, trustees expel Autherine, claiming that she made false charges against them and other University officials.

Dr. Carmichael is a man caught in the middle, hit from all sides with criticism. Some whites do not want African Americans admitted to the University. African Americans are disappointed that Autherine is expelled. Both races complain about the school's failure to discipline those involved in the riots. Some accuse the University of buckling under in favor of mob rule. One student is expelled for his role in the riots; four others are suspended. Wounds are deep, and the healing period is slow.

Dr. Carmichael stays for another year to help the University recover. Then he resigns to undertake an evaluation of higher education in English-speaking countries to be conducted by the Carnegie Foundation. He and Mrs. Carmichael will make their headquarters in Asheville, North Carolina, while traveling back and forth among six countries. I will miss the Carmichaels and hope that I will again have residents as scholarly and gentle as they.

7

Opening Doors to All of Alabama, 1958–1980

Frank A. Rose, 1958–1969

Dr. Carmichael leaves on the last day of 1956, and James H. Newman is named interim president. Dr. Newman and his wife, Dixie, a popular couple in Tuscaloosa, remain in their own home. I stand empty without a family for a year.

Then comes good news. Dr. Frank Anthony Rose, a native Mississippian, is elected president in 1958. He is an ordained minister and comes from the presidency of Transylvania University in Lexington, Kentucky, two striking similarities with our first president, the Reverend Alva Woods. An enthusiastic man of great presence, Dr. Rose had four years earlier been named one of the ten most outstanding young men in the country. His arrival as president is like a burst of fresh spring air on campus, following the trying earlier years.

On April 9, 1958, Dr. Rose is inaugurated. Elaborate ceremonies are planned for Denny Stadium. Some 260 delegates from other colleges and universities attend. Only two other presidents, Alva Woods and Basil Manly, more than one hundred years earlier, had formal inaugurations, so this celebration has real distinction.

Just as the colorfully robed academic procession files into the stadium, a torrential rain drenches everyone. But the showers do not dampen the crowd's spirits. People scurry to Foster Auditorium to continue the ceremony. After the inauguration, the gentlemen attend a luncheon hosted by Dr. Rose, and the ladies go to a separate one given by Mrs. Rose.

Dr. Rose, his wife, Tommye, and four lively youngsters join me. I am excited because I have not had young children living with me since the years of Dr. Denny. The Rose children range in age from two-year-old Elizabeth to fourteen-year-old Susan.

After the Roses move in, hospitable southerners come to call on them. One afternoon Dr. and Mrs. Rose are away and ask Susan to babysit the other three children.

1969 exterior restoration

Office of University Relations

While the Roses are gone, the doorbell rings repeatedly. No one hears it but tiny Elizabeth, who toddles to the door and greets the guests. She invites them inside very properly, climbs into a chair to converse with the two visiting couples, and does not feel awkward at all about having absolutely no clothes on.

No day passes without the need to cope with the energetic Rose children. Tony, ten, and Julian, six, enjoy the women's dorms behind me. Their boyish pranks sometimes draw complaints from the coeds to Dean of Women Sarah Healy that mysterious tomatoes and occasional BB pellets sail into their windows. Mrs. Rose often jokes that the brick wall erected in my backyard is not for their family's privacy but for the students' protection.

Mildred Warner continues her interest in and generosity toward me. She visits Mrs. Rose and talks to her about my dining room. Both ladies agree that I need a large dining room table and at least eight chairs. Mrs. Warner has already spotted a table and chairs, and Mrs. Rose goes to see them. When Mrs. Rose gives her approval, Mrs. Warner makes another gift to me.

In the summer of 1963 two African American students, Vivian Malone and James Hood, apply for summer school. Dr. Rose and his administrators make extensive plans to prepare for the major change. He talks to community leaders and alumni to enlist their aid in public acceptance and a smooth transition.

The sentiment in Tuscaloosa and on campus is that integration is inevitable. But Governor George Wallace does not agree. He notifies United States president John F. Kennedy and Dr. Rose that he will stand in the schoolhouse door, if necessary, to bar the federal government from enforcing a court order to end segregation.

Dr. Rose, President Kennedy, and Attorney General Robert Kennedy talk often. A White House telephone line is installed in a closet in one of my third-floor bedrooms. Even such serious moments have their humor. I get tickled when important people sit on the floor among the skirts of Mrs. Rose's long dresses to use the special telephone. Detailed plans are made for dealing with Governor Wallace's plans.

Dr. Rose does not leave a stone unturned in preparing for this week. He removes every drink machine from campus so that not even a loose bottle will be available to a hothead. He asks all students and faculty who own guns to register them with the campus police. Then he seals off the campus from outsiders. Students, faculty, staff, and work crews must have identification cards to get on campus.

The day of confrontation arrives. From my roof I see heavily armed state highway patrolmen perched on top of Foster Auditorium, where registration will take place.

Vivian Malone, the first African American to graduate from the University of Alabama.
W. S. Hoole Special Collections Library

I hear National Guard helicopters whirling overhead. An anxious crowd gathers in the hot sun to watch the historic event.

Deputy Attorney General Nicholas Katzenbach accompanies the students to registration. They meet Governor Wallace with the state troopers who are standing shoulder to shoulder to form a human barricade. Mr. Katzenbach talks to Governor Wallace and asks him to step aside. Then the governor opens a five-page speech and begins to read. He says he is standing in for thousands of Alabamians who believe the federal government is usurping state power. He will not move and keeps the state troopers beside him.

Mr. Katzenbach takes the students back to their dormitories. After lunch they return to Foster Auditorium. By this time, President Kennedy has federalized the Alabama National Guard. Brigadier General Henry Graham asks Governor Wallace to step aside in compliance with the federal order to admit African Americans. Governor Wallace moves, and Mr. Katzenbach and the two students go inside. Registration then goes smoothly and without further incidents.

Seven years make a dramatic difference on campus. This time it is not necessary for marshals, police, or university administrators to escort the students to class. I see Vivian Malone walking on the quadrangle and chatting with other coeds. James Hood is not as evident, and when I do see him, he is usually alone. Eventually James withdraws from school, but Vivian becomes the first African American graduate of the University.

Another African American, Joffre Whisenton, begins working on his Ph.D. degree at the University, completes all the requirements in 1967, and in 1968 becomes the first African American to receive a doctorate here. The following year his wife, Zadie Bedford Whisenton, receives her Ed.D., and the two hold the distinction of being the first African American couple to receive doctoral degrees from the University.

Homecoming every year is a big affair. Tradition-filled events center around the homecoming football game. Students plan a huge pep rally on the library steps with a bonfire and fireworks. The following morning a long, loud parade with floats and bands marches down University Avenue. Alumni flock to the campus to reminisce, and these celebrations made me happy.

Dr. Rose, like Dr. Denny, sees value in developing a strong sports program. After Dr. Rose came to Alabama, he convinced Paul Bryant, a successful football coach at Texas A&M University, to return to his alma mater. Now we thrill to winning seasons. I relish the sunny fall Saturday afternoons when the campus teems with cheering fans wearing crimson and white colors.

Homecoming in 1963 brings a special event. Susan Rose is getting married. Someone on my ground floor is vacuuming rugs, and another person is polishing furniture in preparation for the wedding. On the second floor my chandeliers are being cleaned with ammonia and water. Suddenly, there is a crash of glass, and I shake from ceiling to floor. My hallway chandelier is on the rug, and a gaping hole is left in my ceiling. What will the Roses do?

Again Mrs. Warner comes to the rescue. "Don't worry, Tommye," she says to Mrs. Rose. "I have several chandeliers in my basement, and I will lend you one."

Fred Maxwell, the University's consulting engineer, suggests ways to replace the plaster molding around the chandelier. He locates a factory-made medallion, and it is matched with the borrowed chandelier. The wedding goes on as scheduled, with Dr. Rose performing the ceremony.

The Roses continue their interest in and good care of me. In 1965 my drawing rooms are redecorated. Fireplaces are painted white, and walls become a soft colonial yellow. Mrs. Rose has a good eye for color, and my new gold draperies are a lovely finishing touch.

The Roses and I host numerous guests. Lady Bird Johnson creates quite a stir when she visits campus to make a speech during her husband's presidency. Such a visitor requires special preparation. Secret Service agents install a direct private telephone line to the White House by boring a hole through my windowsill in the ground-floor bedroom. After all the preparation, though, the White House line gets no use!

Dressed always in a fashionable suit and using his most persuasive voice, Dr. Rose talks about his "vision for greatness" for the University. In speeches on campus and throughout the state, he exercises strong leadership.

My telephones ring early one morning in 1967. Governor Lurleen Wallace and state legislators are upset over *Emphasis '67*, a student publication. The magazine contains an article severely criticizing United States policy in Vietnam and praising the Black Power movement. Legislators protest the use of state funds for publishing such a booklet. Dr. Rose defends the students' right to publish without censorship. He is emphatic that he will quit before he yields to such pressure.

Students rally to Dr. Rose. A petition goes to the legislature with three thousand names. Students then post signs in my yard supporting Dr. Rose. A speaker-ban law aimed at the University fails to pass in an Alabama Senate committee. Dr. Rose's stand for academic freedom is upheld.

By 1967 the Roses decide that major renovations are necessary for me. The architectural firm of McCowan and Knight in Birmingham is selected for the project.

Dr. Rose hired Paul W. "Bear" Bryant in 1958.

W. S. Hoole Special Collections Library

Outbuilding near Rose Administration Building, 1969.
Office of University Relations

Ed McCowan draws plans to enclose the rear porches on my second and third floors. Now I will have a breakfast room on the second floor and a laundry room and a sitting room on the third. Faculty members from the School of Home Economics aid in completely remodeling my kitchen. A new metal staircase from the top floor to the ground is installed to serve as a fire escape, and a carport is added to the back. I am becoming a more practical house for modern family living.

In 1969 Dr. Rose announces his departure for Washington, D.C., to begin his own consulting firm. Trustees name the administration building, now under construction, for him. And the new thirteen-story apartment building for married students will be named for Tommye Rose. She joins Amelia Gayle Gorgas as the second president's wife to have a university building named for her.

I will miss the energetic Rose family. They lived with me longer than any of the other families, except the Manlys and the Dennys. I hope the next residents will love me as much as they did.

F. David Mathews, 1969–1980

Forrest David Mathews, a native of Grove Hill, Alabama, is appointed president to take office in September when Dr. Rose leaves. Dr. Mathews holds two degrees from our university and a Ph.D. degree from Columbia University. He was executive vice president and taught history here earlier. Like Dr. Rose, Dr. Mathews is named one of the ten most outstanding young men in the country by the United States Jaycees. At thirty-three years of age, he is the youngest president of a major university in the country. He is certainly the youngest president I have ever seen.

Dr. Mathews, his wife, Mary, and their daughters, Lee Ann and Lucy, move in. The girls bring a beagle dog with four puppies and two gerbils. I tremble when I hear Mrs. Mathews, even younger than her husband, say to a newspaper reporter, "We don't know much about old houses, but we are willing to learn." I am worried!

The Roses left me in good condition, and the Mathewses are pleased that I am a comfortable place to live. The Maintenance Department believes, however, that my exterior needs painting, and the Mathewses agree. Both Dr. and Mrs. Mathews see me as an important symbol for the state and consider the University a trustee to maintain me for future generations. I am soon surrounded with scaffolding, and work begins.

Then disaster strikes. Paint will not adhere to my plaster, and my old plaster no longer bonds to my bricks. The Mathewses consult with New Orleans historic preservation expert Samuel Wilson, who recommends careful sandblasting, replastering, and painting.

The sandblasting reveals what I have known all along. When the top layer of plaster is removed, another layer of crumbling plaster is found underneath. Having my old face removed and a new one added is a harrowing experience for the Mathewses and for me.

Inside, maintenance workers uncover rotten pine boards beneath the black-and-white tile on my hall floor downstairs. In several places the damp ground underneath can be seen. The boards are removed, and the best ones are saved to put into one of my outbuildings. Then I get new museum-quality dark flooring in the hallway to stand the wear of thousands of annual visitors.

Across my lawn in the new Rose Administration building, Dr. Mathews is busy recruiting administrative leadership. Dr. Raymond McLain, who has been president of both American University in Cairo, Egypt, and Transylvania University in Lexington, Kentucky, becomes academic vice president. Dr. Joseph Sutton, a University alumnus, who has been an administrator at Stetson University, joins him. Dr. Larry McGehee, a protégé of Dr. Rose at Transylvania, and Jim Wilder, a former *Crimson-White* editor, both of whom are close in age to Dr. Mathews, take on major responsibilities. Richard Thigpen, another University alumnus and an outstanding graduate of Yale Law School, soon joins them. The combination of experience and youthful idealism is helpful in what happens next.

Student unrest erupts across the country in 1970. Our campus is no exception. The student deaths at Kent State in Ohio and the Vietnam War generate strong emotions. Across campus, dissidents burn Dressler Hall, an outdated wooden structure. About 125 students are arrested before the unrest subsides.

Dr. Mathews defended academic freedom during the Rose administration and helped defeat a bill that would have barred controversial speakers from campus. He thinks that bringing provocative speakers to campus at this particular time, though, is not wise. He wants invitations deferred until later. About 150 students appear on my lawn at dusk to protest his decision. Dr. Mathews is not home, and Mrs. Mathews assures them that he will see them in his office the following morning. He begins to take walks around the campus to urge calm and speaks to a student rally in Morgan Hall.

Times are difficult. Mrs. Mathews takes Lee Ann and Lucy to spend time away from campus. She dislikes leaving me, but the children's safety is important. When the demonstrations subside, the Mathews trio returns.

Mathews family with huge sign on their lawn on day Dr. Mathews was appointed.

Tuscaloosa News

Like President Wyman, Dr. Mathews is a teacher, and students congregate weekly in the ground-floor study to attend his American history class. Many linger afterward to ask questions and visit.

The Mathewses turn their attention to my grounds. Like my first resident, Mr. Manly, Dr. Mathews keeps careful records of the plants and seasons, and he hires the University's first horticulturalist. Together they draw plans to enhance the natural beauty of the campus. Old shrubbery is moved, and new beds are added. Brick sidewalks line my drive, and a pebble-and-concrete drive replaces my asphalt one.

Visitors to campus compliment the landscape. I enjoy my share of praise from some twenty-five thousand people who visit me annually during tours, open houses, and receptions. Mrs. Mathews's favorite guests are schoolchildren who tour when studying Alabama history. When she needs help to respond to all the requests, a student group called Crimson Girls and Capstone Men assists. Now they and Mrs. Mathews give talks about me to visitors.

A real treasure comes to me in 1971. Mr. and Mrs. Joe Kilgroe of Pell City, Alabama, donate to the University my first piece of Alabama-made furniture. I am so proud of the walnut desk made on a Calhoun County plantation in the early 1800s. Lee Ann and Lucy compose surprise messages for guests and friends to find in the two secret drawers.

January 14, 1972, is a big day for me. I join a host of distinguished buildings across the country on the National Register of Historic Places. I am happy to hold such an honor.

The springtime excitement of the panty raids over the last thirty years is replaced in the early 1970s by a new year-round student fad, streaking! Imagine my surprise when several male students, clad only in tennis shoes, dash across the quadrangle one evening. They hop into a waiting car and ride to a cluster of women's dorms. There they jump out for another run between buildings. The squealing voices of coeds echo around them. Then, like most fads, streaking fades away.

I enjoy seeing national attention come to the University when Dr. Mathews serves as a board member of the Academy for Educational Development and the United States Bicentennial Commission. He cochairs the Southern Growth Policy Board's first Commission on the Future of the South and later chairs the second commission. Mrs. Mathews turns her attention to such local efforts as Lee Ann and Lucy's public schools, the United Way, Tuscaloosa County's Arts and Humanities Council, and the Tombigbee Council of Girl Scouts. She chairs several successful regional fund-raising drives.

Four-year-old Lucy riding her tricycle through the mansion's ground-floor alcove.
Jim Taylor, *Huntsville News*

Mrs. Mathews and Lee Ann sit on canopy bed purchased by Mrs. Gallalee for guest room.

Jim Taylor, *Huntsville News*

In the summer of 1975 United States president Gerald Ford asks Dr. Mathews to join his cabinet as secretary of Health, Education, and Welfare (HEW). After discussing President Ford's request with the trustees, Dr. Mathews takes an eighteen-month leave of absence to serve in Washington. The trustees ask John A. Caddell, president pro tempore of the board, to act as president. Mr. Caddell will not accept the title of acting president but does become the chief executive officer of the University. He meets regularly for several months with Richard Thigpen, now executive vice president at the University and professor in the Law School, and the other vice presidents. After a few months, Mr. Caddell asks to be relieved of his responsibility, and Mr. Thigpen is named chief executive officer until Dr. Mathews returns.

What will happen to me during this time? Mr. Thigpen and his wife, Mary Ann, will continue to live in their own home in Tuscaloosa, and a student will live in the downstairs bedroom while the Mathewses are away, following a tradition of thirty-five years ago. The student will help take care of the house in exchange for a room. The office of Events Coordinator Jean O'Connor also moves to my ground floor. People continue to tour, and social gatherings occur.

While Dr. Mathews is in Washington, the trustees decide to create a systems office for the institutions they oversee in Birmingham, Huntsville, and Tuscaloosa. Joseph F. Volker is named the first chancellor of the system. I will continue to be the residence for the University of Alabama president.

The Mathewses return from Washington in January 1977. Regulations for Title IX, guaranteeing equal opportunity for women in higher education, were written while Dr. Mathews was at HEW. He asks a faculty-student-staff group to begin implementing them here. Initially, the women's athletic program is among the responsibilities of Dr. Joab Thomas, vice president for Student Affairs. Now the planning group envisions a larger program and looks to Coach Paul Bryant for additional funding. Coach Bryant believes that the athletic department should take full responsibility for funding and coordination. The women's program joins his athletic department. Wouldn't Julia Tutwiler be pleased?

The Mathewses entertain guests often. In addition to people from across Alabama, I enjoy seeing such visitors as Norman Cousins, Governor Jay Rockefeller, Senators Edmund Muskie and Edward Kennedy, Jim Nabors, and Joe Namath. When Dr. Mathews invites former president Gerald Ford, the campus bustles with preparation. It is the first time a president of the United States, past or present, has visited the University.

In town and on campus an aura of pride and excitement abounds when President Ford arrives, and I am the hub of all activities for four whole days. He occupies my entire ground floor, and the Secret Service maintains headquarters in one of my outbuildings. No one enters my driveway unless that person's name is on an approved list.

A winning guest, President Ford walks everywhere, much to the students' delight. His days are filled with breakfasts for students and civic leaders and with speeches, meetings, receptions, and dinners. When he leaves, President Ford tells Dr. Mathews, "I have not stayed in such a lovely place since I left the White House." What a wonderful compliment!

After one of Tuscaloosa's heavy rains in 1977, maintenance supervisors find my rear flat-roofed carport leaking profusely and deteriorating rapidly. Dr. Mathews designs a curved, wooden canopy–type replacement, and the University carpenters build it. The new carport complements the archway in my back alcove and is trimmed in matching latticework.

Dr. Mathews hopes the University will be a leader in confronting the complex issues facing Alabama and the South. Faculty and students work with southern governors and experts throughout the region who are trying to create a "New South." To extend the University's accessibility, officials open centers in major cities across the state.

New academic divisions spring up across the campus. Dr. Mathews secures legislative funding for a College of Community Health Sciences, created to respond to the health care crisis in rural Alabama, and for the School of Mines and Energy Development, established to promote responsible development of Alabama's mineral wealth. He is especially proud of the faculty who develop programs for disabled children, and the Center for Emotionally Disturbed children is created to further their work.

Dr. Mathews sees the end of segregation as a time for the University to reach out to all of Alabama and create new programs that will reposition our institution in society. He thinks it particularly important that students learn from these changes by being directly involved in them.

Minority enrollment increases rapidly, and black scholars join the faculty. Dr. Mathews and Dr. Harold Stinson, president of Stillman College, collaborate to create a joint position to be held by Dr. Joffre Whisenton. Dr. Whisenton will work 60 percent of the time as a faculty member at Stillman and 40 percent of the time at the University on the Student Development staff. He, Dr. Stinson, and Dr. Mathews develop an exchange program between the two institutions for library use, class enrollment, and extracurricular activities. In 1969 Dr. Mathews also recruits Haywood L. Strickland, an African American professor at Stillman, to teach the first course in black history at the University.

Also in 1969, Wendell Hudson is the first African American to sign a basketball scholarship here, and Wilbur Jackson follows him in football the following year. The campus buzzes in 1973 when Governor George Wallace crowns Terry Points, the first African American to be elected homecoming queen. Cleo Thomas is the first African American student to be elected president of the Student Government Association. He will hold that office for the 1976–77 school year.

The president supports the Honors Program, a degree-granting New College, and campus internships for students. He also begins a faculty internship program for young faculty, which attracts a young political scientist named Malcolm Portera, later to become chancellor of the University System. More colleges are added to broaden and strengthen the University academically. They include the Graduate School of Library Science, the School of Communication, and the Capstone College of Nursing.

New buildings go up. The Ferguson Center, named for long-time trustee Hill Ferguson, the College of Community Health Sciences complex, and a new law center are added. Woods Hall and other old friends of mine are restored, and a twelve-acre nationally registered historic district is established.

Dr. Mathews also encourages research in international business projects and travels to Japan to open doors for the University. Japanese visitors—everyone from Ambassador and Mrs. Fumihiko Togo to Japan's educators and business leaders—arrive on campus. They are amazed at the similarities of vegetation, climate, and traditions with their own country. But they are even more surprised to discover that Dr. Mathews plants Japanese perilla and mitsuba in my flower beds!

The Mathews decade is one of rapid changes and expansion and, with these, controversy. In the fall of 1979 the University is faced with a sudden drop in legislative appropriations. Members of the faculty are concerned and approach the trustees. Salary increases and more direct participation in the selection of deans and department heads are among the topics. Dr. Mathews responds in a detailed report and meets with faculty across campus. Delaying maintenance, along with other cost-cutting measures, enables the University to save enough money to increase salaries.

Nearly every day I hear Mrs. Mathews click-clacking on the typewriter at her rolltop desk near the window in my third-floor hallway, her favorite place to work. I watch as she writes the stories she has learned about me while living here. Lucy compiles a book of photographs and drawings showing how I have looked since I was built. A publisher is interested in printing Mrs. Mathews's manuscript. Imagine that!

During the summer of 1980, the Mathewses leave. Dr. Mathews resigns as president to head the National Consortium for Public Policy Education in Washington, D.C., and shortly afterward becomes president of the Kettering Foundation in Dayton, Ohio. I will miss the spirited, active Mathews family and all of the pets and students I met.

On July 1 Dr. Howard Gundy is named acting president of the University. Having already served as a dean and academic vice president here, he is an experienced administrator. Dr. Gundy and his wife, Janet, continue to live in their home in Tuscaloosa while he serves for one year.

8

Fostering Research and Restoration, 1981–2003

Joab L. Thomas, 1981–1988

In March 1981 the trustees announce the selection of Joab Langston Thomas as the new president. Dr. Thomas, an outstanding native Alabamian with three degrees from Harvard University, had previously been a biology professor and a vice president at the University of Alabama. He is an authority on plants and is a coauthor of a book about wildflowers in Alabama and the southeastern states. He comes to us now from the chancellorship of North Carolina State University, where he was a popular administrator.

Friends and relatives welcome Dr. Thomas, his wife, Marly, and their children home again. Catherine will be a sophomore at Harvard; David will be a freshman at the University; Jennifer and Frances will go to schools in Tuscaloosa.

The Thomases are encouraged to live in a recently updated University-owned house in a nearby residential neighborhood. They appreciate my significance and historic structure, but with increasing state proration (pro rata reductions), there are no funds for repairs for me. I regret not having the presidential family live with me, but I will continue to be the center for official entertaining.

Dr. Thomas hopes to make the University a great research institution. He sees this as a way to develop faculty talents and to assist in the state's overall economic development. A lean economic year with proration of state funds as high as 10 percent challenge that goal, but Dr. Thomas continues. He strengthens student admission and retention standards and establishes a comprehensive core curriculum. He urges the faculty to increase their research and publication efforts.

In 1983 our University makes the front page of the *New York Times* with good news. The newspaper reports that the University assisted in saving the Rochester Products plant in Tuscaloosa from closing. Just last fall, General Motors, for whom Rochester Products makes carburetors, the United Automobile Workers union, and

Tuscaloosa community leaders asked the University for help. Several factories had already closed, leaving the community battling inflation and high unemployment rates. The University agreed to send students and faculty into the Rochester Products plant in an experimental program. Dr. Barry Mason, dean of the University's College of Commerce and Business Administration, chairs the group. Over a three-year period, the innovators will try to identify cost savings and to streamline operations. All agreed that the plant would stay open if a certain level of cost savings could be reached. An annual savings of $470,000 is identified even before the study is completed.

Because of the good results with Rochester Products, Stockham Valve and Fittings Company in Birmingham signs a similar agreement with the University for assistance. I smile with Dr. Thomas that the University is playing an economic development role, just as he had hoped.

Dr. Thomas and Dr. John Blackburn, vice president for development, continue plans made earlier for a big fund-raising campaign. They name it the Capital Campaign for Academic Achievement. A feasibility study had not encouraged the goal that the University set, so everyone is happy when the campaign raises $62 million, almost twice the established goal. The successful campaign is a great tribute to the fund-raising pair and to the reputation of the University.

Dignitaries continue to visit the campus, and the Thomases always entertain them with a reception or dinner with me. Former United States presidents Gerald Ford and Jimmy Carter speak on campus. President Ronald Reagan, Senator John Glenn and his wife, Annie, and Henry Kissinger all participate in special programs.

Meanwhile, wonderful aromas are wafting through my kitchen. Mmmm. Mrs. Thomas often cooks in my big kitchen for University guests and enjoys using family recipes. The large, extended Thomas family is renowned for its excellent cooks and the food served at annual family reunions. Mrs. Thomas encourages family members in collecting recipes and publishing them. She serves as the editor of *Family Secrets*, a comprehensive cookbook. Proceeds from the cookbook assist in the upkeep of the William Henry Thomas family home in Bibb County, Alabama. The book is a huge success and even has two printings in its first year. When people now eat something special here that Mrs. Thomas cooks from the book, they can find the recipe easily.

Mrs. Thomas continues to contribute her time to the community. Before moving to North Carolina, she had been the president of the Tuscaloosa Junior League, and now she chairs the American Red Cross board.

In August 1985 I am excited to be part of happy wedding plans. The oldest Thomas daughter, Catherine, is marrying Dr. Robert McGee, Jr. The bridesmaids will spend the night with me before the wedding. The entire family is involved. Jennifer and Frances are bridesmaids, and David is the trumpeter in the ceremony at Christ Episcopal Church downtown. A wonderful reception takes place here after the wedding. I like these festive occasions.

The following year Dr. Thomas leads in actively recruiting Japanese industry. Japan Victor Corporation (JVC) decides to locate a plant in Tuscaloosa to assemble videocassette tapes. Shortly afterward, JVC announces it will also make compact discs here.

The Alabama Industrial Development Authority (AIDA), inspired by the JVC success, decides to open an office in Japan. The director of the AIDA office is from Narashino City, Japan, and, coincidentally, so is the chief executive officer of JVC. Tuscaloosans are excited when the mayor of Narashino City accepts an invitation to visit. Dr. and Mrs. Thomas host a dinner in his honor in my dining room. Dr. Thomas and the Japanese mayor toast one another warmly. The Japanese enjoy southern hospitality and establish a sister city relationship between Narashino City and Tuscaloosa.

The Chronicle of Higher Education in 1986 names Dr. Thomas as one of twenty-nine of the nation's most effective college presidents of research and doctoral-degree granting institutions. He is the only one from the Deep South. I am proud.

Dr. Thomas works on academic enhancements and establishes a Presidential Scholars Program to give awards to 150 students each year. The University sees an increase in the number of National Merit scholars. The Honors Program is expanded University-wide.

I enjoy seeing prospective students come to campus. The Crimson Girls and Capstone Men bring them on tours and to receptions to see me. I think of myself as a recruiter also.

The University's academic achievements continue to grow. External support for research more than triples, and eleven new endowed faculty chairs are established during the Thomas administration.

Simultaneously, sports require a lot of our president's time. Dr. Thomas appreciates and understands the role of sports. He played football, baseball, basketball, and track—every sport his high school provided. The University had offered him a football scholarship when he graduated from high school, but he decided to attend Harvard and concentrate on his studies.

Dr. and Mrs. Thomas entertain Senator and Mrs. John Glenn.

Chip Cooper, Office of University Relations

Paul Bryant, who coached football here for twenty-five years and won six national championships, retires in December, just a little over a year after Dr. Thomas's arrival. Dr. Thomas faces a huge challenge to replace the nationally respected Coach Bryant. Ray Perkins follows Coach Bryant and does well, but he decides to leave to accept the head coaching position with a professional team. Then Bill Curry becomes the head coach. Coach Curry has not previously had Alabama ties, and some football fans are often not kind to him, but Alabama continues to field winning teams.

The College Football Association (CFA) elects Dr. Thomas as its president. CFA promotes guidelines for academic standards, recruiting, and scholarship allotments. David Thomas attends almost as many sports-related events as his father because he plays in the Million Dollar Band, the University's marching band, for three years and then becomes a cheerleader in his senior year.

Dr. Thomas oversees new construction and growth on campus. The new Frank Moody Music Building becomes a cultural center for campus. Dr. Thomas secures funding and approvals for a new science library. The alumni and friends of Coach Bryant are interested in seeing his legacy memorialized, and several new structures bear his name. The Bryant Alumni–Continuing Education Center is completed. The Bryant Museum opens in an adjacent building and immediately begins attracting visitors to campus. Denny Stadium is enlarged, and trustees vote to add Coach Bryant's name to it, making it Bryant-Denny Stadium.

In 1988 Dr. Thomas and the University receive recognition again. Dr. Thomas is named one of the top ten university presidents in the category titled Comprehensive Doctoral Granting Institutions by a research study conducted by Ohio scholars. I am as proud as a mother hen.

For seven years now, Dr. Thomas has been president of the University, following five as chancellor of North Carolina State University and seven previously as a university administrator. He never expected to be out of the classroom for nineteen years and decides that he would like to return to the classroom and teach biology. Trustees vote to give him a two-semester sabbatical. He and Mrs. Thomas spend a semester at North Carolina State University, where Dr. Thomas devotes his time to reviewing the rapid changes in the field of biology. He returns to Tuscaloosa to continue research and to work on a book on poisonous plants. The following year, Dr. Thomas teaches two courses at the University and finishes his contribution to *Poisonous Plants and Venomous Animals of Alabama.*

As much as Dr. Thomas loves teaching, he decides to accept another administrative challenge. In July 1990 Penn State University names Dr. Thomas its new president. Dr. and Mrs. Thomas will move to Pennsylvania so he can begin his duties in September. I will miss seeing the Thomases. Both of them always approached their tasks with optimism and enthusiasm.

E. Roger Sayers, 1988–1996

When Dr. Thomas leaves the presidency in 1988, Dr. Earl Roger Sayers, a native of Illinois and a graduate of the University of Illinois, is named acting president. He earned M.A. and Ph.D. degrees from Cornell and has been at our University for more than twenty-five years. Like Dr. Thomas, Dr. Sayers began his career here in the Biology Department before serving in several administrative capacities. He has been academic vice president since 1980 and is a natural to fill this interim position.

As acting president, Dr. Sayers sees his role as continuing the initiatives begun during the previous administration. In an early speech, he emphasizes that he will enhance the quality of academic programs, strengthen the total research capacity, and assist the state with economic development.

Dr. and Mrs. Sayers have a home in Tuscaloosa and continue to live there, so I am still without a family. I will be a focus for campus events, but I need attention to interior and exterior problems that have been developing.

During Dr. Sayers's year as acting president, football coach Bill Curry leaves, and Dr. Sayers moves ahead to hire a new coach, Gene Stallings, and names Cecil ("Hootie") Ingram the new athletic director. Many are thrilled that they both have Alabama ties, and the two are accepted immediately.

At the end of 1988, trustees ask Dr. Sayers to move from acting president to become the president of the University. He will begin his duties with the new year. I am thrilled when I hear the trustees encourage Dr. Sayers and his wife, MarLa, to live with me.

The Sayers certainly want to live with me if I can be made livable. I need a lot of work. The last big interior design changes were made during the Rose administration almost four decades ago. The last major exterior work was done when the Mathews family lived with me, again a long time ago. For nine years I have been unoccupied.

Dr. Sayers tells the trustees that he would like to see private money raised for my renovation. A committee of three, MarLa Sayers, Jean Hinton, and Cecil Williams, all from Tuscaloosa, go to work. Mrs. Sayers and Mrs. Hinton are both graduates of the University, and Mrs. Williams is the wife of one of the trustees. Sandee Gibson

Dr. and Mrs. Sayers with the Mansion's 150th anniversary cake.

Chip Cooper, Office of University Relations

and Dr. John Blackburn in the Development Office provide good counsel. With such a powerful team, the group raises almost $700,000 for me. What great news!

Mrs. Sayers goes to work on my kitchen immediately. With the large-scale entertaining that happens here, I need to be much more efficient. I get a brand new look. Commercial stove tops and ovens, warmers, and freezers make entertaining more convenient. Over time I have come a long way from the day when my kitchen was in one of the outbuildings.

The state of Alabama is fortunate to have the respected historic preservation architect Nicholas Holmes in Mobile, Alabama, and he is contacted for advice. He addresses my infrastructure and says it is imperative to do basic tasks first. The roof, plumbing, wiring, and heating and cooling systems all need updating. Outside drainage is a problem. My basement continues to be damp.

Scaffolding springs up, saws buzz, and dust swirls. Mr. Holmes sets strict guidelines for the University's Maintenance Department to follow as the crews work. Carefully preserving the integrity of my structure, Mr. Holmes sensitively locates new pipes, ducts, and outlets. He works on water problems by installing a new system of French drains. Then he enlists North Carolinian George T. Fore, a historical-paint consultant, to analyze paint samples with the goal of identifying some of my original interior wall colors. Mr. Fore takes paint samples from the walls of the state capitol in Montgomery at the same time he works on my colors. I do not mind any of the activity and am quite content with the work being done.

Allison Bailey, an interior designer from Decatur, Alabama, joins the team to make me elegant. He is good with colors. He and Mrs. Sayers select fabrics to re-cover the furniture in the drawing rooms. Mrs. Sayers replaces the threadbare carpet and the dark flooring on the ground floor with wide pine boards and handsome Oriental rugs she has purchased. She also shops for furniture for the ground floor.

Visitors who will stay with me in the ground-floor bedroom will enjoy the renovation results. Everything from wallpaper to draperies to furniture is replaced. The biggest change, though, is that the accompanying bathroom is enlarged with modern equipment. The new Jacuzzi would surprise my early residents, who had no such indoor plumbing.

Then Mrs. Sayers and Sandee Gibson have an idea. They decide to add an Oriental runner to the handsome curved stairway with an accompanying decorative brass rod at each step. Ann Adams Pritchard and Lella Clayton Bromberg, both University alumnae now living in Birmingham, Alabama, assist in identifying people who might like to honor someone through a stairway memorial gift. The University of

Alabama Alumni Association is the first to participate in this effort and honors two presidents' wives: Louise Garland, who saved me during the Civil War, and MarLa Sayers, who is addressing my renovation.

Dr. and Mrs. Sayers travel to Hungary on a trip associated with the University's Office of International Programs. There Mrs. Sayers continues to think about me. She purchases a handsome banquet-sized tablecloth with matching place mats and napkins to be used for special occasions. My guests will be impressed with the elegant table appointments.

Frances Summersell, the widow of much-loved University History Department chairman Dr. Charles Summersell, gives some beautiful family antiques. Colonel William D. Stone, a University trustee and member of my original building committee, was a relative of Mrs. Summersell's. She and her cousin, Dora Going, donate a copy of a portrait of Mr. Stone that has been in her family for several generations. She also designates valuable early 1800s furniture, an Oriental rug, and a French gold leaf mirror to come to me. The Summersells' treasures have become my treasures.

Mrs. Marguerite Smith Turner from Anniston, Alabama, a relative of President Landon Garland, donates a love seat that belonged to the Garlands and a portrait of Dr. Garland. I am delighted to see the love seat return to me.

Dr. and Mrs. Sayers are concerned about the cost of upkeep for me, and so is Mrs. Ella Richardson Davis of Tuscaloosa. Mrs. Davis establishes an endowment at one of the local banks to generate money for special projects for me. The generosity of others directly affects my well-being, and I realize how fortunate I am.

The infrastructure updates and decorative remodeling take almost a year to complete. By this time I have waited more than a decade for a family. At last Dr. and Mrs. Sayers move in. Their adult children are already living elsewhere and will return to visit. I am as lighthearted as a student after passing a tough exam and ready to celebrate.

The University is ready to celebrate also. Two days of festivities are planned for April 12–13, 1991, my 150th birthday. The School of Library Science's Book Arts Program, one of only two such programs in the United States for book and paper making, prepares a handsome book with handmade paper to record the participants in the renovation. Many donors happily return to be recognized. I will never forget the weekend, the wonderfully generous people, and especially the big birthday cake!

Mrs. Sayers, Mrs. Hinton, and Mrs. Williams, who worked so diligently for my restoration, now organize more formally. The first Mansion Renovation Committee is established, with some additional members added to the group. Dr. Jerry Oldshue,

University archivist, becomes an ex officio member. The group sets guidelines both for architectural and decorative changes to me and for groups who want to use my lawn or me for an event. I feel protected and appreciated.

I relish hearing the compliments I receive every day now. The Sayerses clearly like living with me, and I am elated to have a family again. Mrs. Sayers also recruits a committee of talented volunteers who prepare dramatic flower arrangements for special events. Guests talk about and remember the spectacular bouquets.

Student neighbors surround me. One day a young man from the nearby scholarship dorm stops by to borrow the proverbial cup of sugar. Mrs. Sayers is surprised and delighted when he returns later with a warm cupcake he has baked.

A faulty hidden light switch in the floor of a third-floor bedroom gives us all a scare. The switch had been installed in the floor above the dining room about fifty years ago to highlight a painting over the mantel. The minute switch did not appear on any of the drawings when the wiring was reworked. No one knew it was there until the carpet in the bedroom above the dining room began to smoke.

Dr. Sayers sees the smoke from his office in the Rose Administration Building, and he responds with the fire department to the alarm. Quick-thinking firemen rip up the smoldering carpet and throw it out of the third-floor window. Whew! What a fright! Fortunately, the fire is contained quickly, with smoke fumes providing the only damage to me.

People continue to give antiques to the University and to me. Dr. and Mrs. William Price from Birmingham, Alabama, donate handsome pieces of furniture and decorative items. Mrs. Marie Ingalls, also from Birmingham, gives a beautiful twelve-piece place setting of sterling silver. Lovely gifts like these will attract other handsome contributions.

As president, Dr. Sayers continues his role as implementer. His leadership guides in strengthening admissions standards and emphasizing academic achievement. He oversees the construction of buildings that had been in the planning stages earlier. The Eric and Sarah Rodgers Science Library and the Tom Bevill Energy, Mineral, and Materials Science Research Building are dedicated in 1990. Mary Hewell Alston Hall for commerce and business is dedicated the next year.

Dr. Sayers undertakes the largest capital campaign in the history of the University. This time the goal is $225 million. Funds for endowed chairs and permanent endowment are included in the campaign, as well as support for new buildings. The campus is jubilant when the goal is handily exceeded, and I am ecstatic also.

Sports activities are fun for Dr. and Mrs. Sayers, and they attend many events. The football team under Coach Stallings wins a national championship in 1992. Other records follow. The baseball team goes to the College World Series. The women's gymnastic team wins two national championships. The men's and women's basketball teams consistently do well.

Following the model of recruiting Japanese industry to Tuscaloosa, Dr. Sayers and one of the vice presidents, Dr. Malcolm Portera, collaborate with the city and the state to attract Mercedes-Benz to the community. They had learned earlier in trying to lure a Saturn plant to the area what was needed to be successful. In 1993 there is great excitement when Mercedes-Benz selects Tuscaloosa to locate its first factory outside of Germany to build passenger vehicles. The huge manufacturing plant adds vitality to Tuscaloosa's economy, and I wonder whether I will see more people in Mercedes vehicles drive by me now.

Dr. Sayers now begins his own initiatives. New construction is planned. The Bruno Business Library is dedicated in 1994, and the Sloan Bashinsky Computer Center on the first floor of the building is also dedicated that same year. Mary Harmon Bryant Hall is planned and built. An addition is added to the Student Recreation Center and to the Tom Bevill Building. Dr. Sayers begins discussion about a new building across from the Bevill complex.

Every president who lives with me faces controversies. The Student Government Association (SGA) has a series of difficult elections in which some candidates are targets of violence. Dr. Sayers explains that it is time for decisive action when violence takes place on campus. He disbands the SGA in 1993 and encourages students to rethink the way campus governance is organized.

Students decide to hold a constitutional convention, and a representative from every registered student organization on campus is invited to attend. They meet and, after much discussion, divide into subcommittees for executive, legislative, and judicial functions. Then they work together for eighteen months. One student, Jessica Medeiros, acts as recording secretary for all three groups. At the end of the process, she is asked to combine the ideas and reports into one document, a new constitution, for review.

When the document is ready, the students plan a referendum to approve it. Everyone agrees that voter turnout must meet a minimum percentage for the document to be approved. On election day, the turnout more than exceeds the minimum, and the constitution is approved in the spring of 1996. I hear the huge celebration that takes place on campus when the election results are announced.

Dr. Sayers is proud of the students for staying engaged in the process over such a long period of time. The students are also proud of what they have accomplished. In the fall, the first election of the reestablished SGA is held. I am not surprised when Jessica Medeiros is elected president.

Dr. Sayers finds that he has to spend a great deal of time with inquiries from the National Collegiate Athletic Association (NCAA). He is relieved when the University wins a successful appeal of a ruling by an NCAA infractions committee, the first time ever that an NCAA infractions ruling has been overturned. The inquiry process remains open, though, and continues to be an ongoing distraction.

Just as his predecessors were challenged by state proration, Dr. Sayers also faces cutbacks. I see how painful it is to adapt, without much advance warning, to cutbacks three different times during his administration.

Dr. Sayers works hard to unite the University and the town. He is the first University president to serve as president of the local chamber of commerce. He also reaches out to the state by expanding the President's Cabinet and building a broad coalition. Mrs. Sayers follows his lead and serves on the boards of the local AIDS Foundation and the statewide American Cancer Society. She also volunteers for two terms as president of the board of the University Club.

The eight years as president and eight before that as academic vice president have been full ones for Dr. Sayers. In 1996 he decides to retire. He and Mrs. Sayers buy the Tuscaloosa home of Jeff Coleman, who was associated with our University for more than fifty years, and move there.

I will always be obliged to the Sayerses for the restoration and wonderful care they gave me. Dr. Sayers was a sound administrator, and both he and Mrs. Sayers made many long-lasting friends for the University and for me.

Andrew A. Sorensen, 1996–2002

Dr. Andrew Aaron Sorensen, a native of Pittsburgh, becomes president of the University in the summer of 1996. He has been provost and vice president of academic affairs at the University of Florida. I am already impressed with all of his earned degrees. He holds a bachelor's degree in divinity and both a master's degree and a doctoral degree in medical sociology from Yale University. He also earned a bachelor's degree in history from the University of Illinois and a master's degree in public health from the University of Michigan.

Dr. and Mrs. Sorensen

Chip Cooper, Office of University Relations

Dr. Sorensen and his wife, Donna, move in with me right away. They have two grown sons, Aaron and Ben, who are already on their own. Mrs. Sorensen believes that the president's wife determines my personality and that the president determines the institution's personality. She sees me as a warm, inviting place and works to promote that image for me.

The Sorensens appreciate the splendid condition in which Dr. and Mrs. Sayers left me and have only a few minor adjustments to make. Every family has to address, in some way, the circulation issues that plague me, and the Sorensens identify problems to be corrected to the air handling system. Some additional lighting is added on my third floor.

Then I am treated to something I have not had in a long time—outdoor furniture on my second-floor front porch. Dr. Sorensen likes to sit on the porch and read the newspaper. When people see him reading outside, they often stop to visit. Parents discuss various concerns, such as that their children will not be able to get into the University or that they may face academic problems. Students stop by to chat. One day an architect and his young son appear on the porch, and Dr. Sorensen gives them a tour of me. He does not see the quick visits as interruptions.

The University begins planning Dr. Sorensen's inaugural activities, the first formal inauguration since Dr. Rose was president. Dr. Sorensen finds himself in a position that others might view as a challenge, but he sees it as a unique opportunity to connect with the past. Two former University presidents, Dr. Thomas and Dr. Sayers, and two former acting presidents, Dr. Thigpen and Dr. Gundy, all continue to live in Tuscaloosa. Dr. Mathews works in another state. Dr. Sorensen invites all of them to be a part of the inaugural festivities.

The inauguration on October 18, 1996, is an auspicious occasion indeed. All five of the former presidents and many representatives from other colleges and universities attend. The ceremony is held in Sellers Auditorium of the Bryant Conference Center on campus. Speakers bring greetings from various groups. Trustee Emeritus Winton M. ("Red") Blount is the primary guest speaker. He announces a $7 million gift from his family and the Blount Foundation, designated for the Undergraduate Initiative Program, a plan designed for the College of Arts and Sciences to integrate the learning experience into the residential setting. This is the largest gift ever received by the College of Arts and Sciences and has already attracted other gifts from individuals and foundations to support the program.

Dr. Sorensen uses words emblazoned on Bibb Graves Hall to connect his vision for the University's future with its past: "Religion, morality and knowledge being

At President Sorensen's inauguration, left to right: Howard Gundy, Andrew Sorensen, Joab Thomas, David Mathews, Roger Sayers, and Richard Thigpen.

Chip Cooper, Office of University Relations

necessary to good government and the happiness of mankind, schools and the means of education shall forever be encouraged." He outlines hopes for strengthening research, offering a distinctive education at an affordable price, and rewarding faculty members for their work.

Not long after the Sorensens move in with me, Jack Warner and Elizabeth, his wife, join them for lunch. Mr. Warner, the retired chairman and chief executive officer of Gulf States Paper Corporation, which is headquartered in Tuscaloosa, is the son of Mildred Warner, who first began buying antiques for me during the Carmichael administration. Mr. Warner and his company own a fabulous collection of art and antiques, and he and his wife are friends of the University.

During lunch, the discussion turns to furnishings in my dining room. Mrs. Sorensen innocently asks Mr. Warner whether he thinks the chandelier is too small for the room. Mr. Warner responds immediately that it certainly is too little. He has the perfect Waterford chandelier, one that he considers more in scale for the size of the room, in storage. Soon afterward, the magnificent chandelier arrives at my door, complete with a person to install it properly.

Mrs. Sorensen describes the chandelier as the beginning of Mr. Warner's "vision with legs that ran and ran." Another exceptional Waterford chandelier appears for the drawing room. Mr. Warner travels to auction houses throughout the world looking for fine, exquisite pieces that he considers appropriate for me. A dining room table with matching chairs, pier mirrors, and a splendid sideboard are just a few of the antiques he locates. He continues with accessories, new wallpaper, new draperies, and new paint colors.

Mr. Warner says, "Any truly great university should have a gem that lifts the soul above the clouds," and it is apparent that he wants me to be that gem. I am quite an elegant house when he finishes.

An assistant professor, Shirley Foster, receives a grant so she and her students can catalog the new furnishings. They produce a handsome booklet of the Warner collection. Sandee Gibson Kirby meticulously maintains an inventory of the gifts and where they are placed.

The best news of all comes when I hear Mr. Warner say he would like to recreate my balustrade. He discusses the project with Dr. Sorensen, who has had extensive preservation experience as president of the board of the Preservation Institute: Nantucket, operated by the University of Florida. Dr. Sorensen writes to Dr. Robert Mellown, a well-known University professor who is an authority on historic architecture, particularly mine, for advice about my balustrade and the restoration of other historic buildings on campus. The two men consult with Harvie P. Jones, a Huntsville, Alabama, architect, who is considered by many to be the foremost preservation architect in the southeastern United States.

Mr. Jones realizes what a complicated project this will be because there are no drawings of the original roof balustrade. Fortunately for me, he is a persistent researcher. The earliest graphic showing the balustrade is an 1840s watercolor painting. Although some of the details are sketchy, the painting appears to show my true proportions.

Dr. Mellown supplies historic photographs of the 1834 Dearing home and the 1829 capitol, both located in Tuscaloosa and both of which originally had roof balustrades. A man is standing under the balustrade line in the Dearing photo; Mr. Jones uses known dimensions of the Dearing home and the man to recheck the proportions and measurements of that balustrade to compare with the measurements he has calculated for me. He determines that eighteen inches is my original balustrade height. It feels right to me.

Next, Mr. Jones talks with an architect from the National Park Service in Washington, D.C., about appropriate materials and the cost. Four different materials are recommended. Honduras mahogany is selected, and the new balustrade is made and installed with the drawings Mr. Jones provides.

Alas, woods are no longer the slow-growing, enduring ones of the past, and super-protective lead paint is no longer allowed. The same fate of the original wooden balustrade now befalls this one. The wood splits and begins to rot. I am disappointed, but thank goodness, Mr. Warner is undaunted.

Synthetic materials are used in the Alabama capitol restoration in Montgomery and in portions of some National Park Service installations across the country. Mr. Warner works with University architect Hugh Kilpatrick and Tim Harrison of Tuscaloosa and decides to try fiberglass. Mr. Jones insists that a mold be made of a portion of the mahogany reproduction to maintain the correct dimensions. An exact duplicate in fiberglass is made and installed in 1997.

After all the hard work, everyone is pleased with the result. I surely have a balanced look once again, and I am hopeful that this balustrade will be with me for quite a long time.

On a sunny Alabama day in June 2000, Dr. Sorensen greets more than two hundred guests who attend the groundbreaking for an interdisciplinary science center. He has been involved in the development of this building from its inception through all the approvals. The center is being named for Senator Richard Shelby and his wife, Dr. Annette N. Shelby, and it will be one of the largest buildings on our campus. It is a happy day, with members of the Shelby family participating in all the activities. Dr. Sorensen announces that the building will be completed in 2002.

In September 2000, Winton and Carolyn Blount return to campus for the festive dedication of the Blount Initiative Living-Learning Center. The center is designed to enhance the four-year special liberal arts program for selected students within the College of Arts and Sciences.

Good news arrives from Mercedes-Benz U.S. International in October. The company pledges a $1 million endowment fund to be used primarily to expand an existing student cooperative education program. The Sorensens invite officials of the company to visit me.

The University receives more exciting news. *U.S. News and World Report* is listing the University among the top fifty public universities in the country. Funds for external research are doubled. The millennium is turning out to be quite a splendid year.

In addition to new projects, Dr. Sorensen is affected by the work of his predecessors. The Alabama Institute for Manufacturing Excellence building, begun earlier during the Sayers administration, is dedicated in 2000. Mary Harmon Bryant Hall, also completed earlier, is dedicated in 2001. The Alabama State Oil and Gas Board, the Geological Survey of Alabama, and many of the Museum of Natural History's collections are housed here. I have to admit I am partial to this building because it preserves so many of my records and photographs.

Our University libraries are also a favorite of Mrs. Sorensen. She works with Dr. Charles Osburn, dean of University Libraries, to found the *Rotunda Library Society*, which promotes annual giving and library awareness, and serves as the first chair of the Library Leadership Board. She is quite touched later when a library endowment is established in her honor to feature the contributions of southern women.

Mrs. Sorensen is also quite active in the community and serves on several local and regional boards. She takes boardsmanship seriously on the Big Brothers–Big Sisters board and becomes a big sister herself to a six-year-old. She and Dr. Sorensen develop a relationship with the youngster that lasts far beyond her board term. I find it rewarding to have young people visit with me, too.

Another continuing issue is the ongoing investigation of the football team by the NCAA. Dr. Sorensen and his legal team spend a huge amount of time sorting through documents and interviews. I see the enormous distraction and distress for our president, the heartache for the alumni, the sadness of the students, and the disappointment for the young athletes. I hope this will end soon.

Dr. Sorensen, an avid bike rider, peddles about the campus in the early morning hours. His usual route is the perimeter around campus, and he observes details from his bicycle that he might not see otherwise. One of the vice presidents jokingly tells Dr. Sorensen that he is thinking of puncturing his bike tires so he will not get so many memos after the president's dawn rides.

Continuing his interest in historic preservation, Dr. Sorensen supports work on the exterior and interior of the Gorgas House and the exteriors and interiors of Tuomey and Barnard halls, the latter two to be used as part of the Blount Living-Learning Center. The Student Recreation Center is expanded. With trustee Thomas Rast and the facilities planning group, Dr. Sorensen lays plans for a residential retirement community to be built on University land by a private developer.

I hear Mrs. Sorensen reminiscing about many of the guests we have entertained. She enjoys the students, faculty, politicians, actors, and business people who visit me. In keeping with her love of libraries, Mrs. Sorensen finds that her favorite guests are Alabama authors Nelle Harper Lee and Kathryn Tucker Windham.

In May 2002 Dr. Sorensen presides over his last commencement. In July he will become president of the University of South Carolina. He and Mrs. Sorensen will leave me and move into another historic president's home, a mid-1800s house on the Horseshoe of the Columbia, South Carolina, campus. I will miss them and like to think that I have given them good experiences for their next challenge of living in and appreciating an old house located in the middle of a college campus.

Dr. Barry Mason, dean of the Culverhouse College of Commerce and Business Administration at the University, is named acting president. He and his wife, Linda, will remain in their own home in Tuscaloosa.

J. Barry Mason (acting), 2002–2003

Dr. Joseph Barry Mason has already had a distinguished career as a professor, department chair, and dean of the College of Commerce and Business Administration. He completed his undergraduate work at Louisiana Tech University and earned a doctoral degree at Alabama, after which he has served this institution for thirty-five years.

Dr. Malcolm Portera is now chancellor of the University of Alabama System. He also has had a long history with us, having served as executive assistant to two presidents, as a vice president, and as vice chancellor of external affairs of the

University of Alabama System. He led his undergraduate alma mater, Mississippi State University, as its sixteenth president in the late 1990s before returning to Tuscaloosa to become chancellor of the University system.

Now Dr. Portera meets with Dr. Mason and sets some explicit expectations. He tells Dr. Mason that he and the trustees will support a vigorous acting president and do not want to go through a year of suspended development.

Dr. Mason addresses several issues immediately. He learns that our University is the only school in the Southeastern Conference that has local bars open twenty-four hours every day of the week. He begins what is called the Healthy Campus Initiative with a coalition of diverse constituencies who successfully lower the number of open bar hours. The group also works to educate students about lifestyle choices, to plan weekend recreational activities, and to establish better relations with the city of Tuscaloosa and the neighborhoods.

The Neighborhood Partnership grows out of the Healthy Campus Initiative. A broad coalition of city council members, students, police officers, judicial affairs representatives, campus planners, neighborhood residents, and outside constituents join forces to bring stability to the adjacent campus neighborhoods. The multifaceted group is committed to working long term on neighborhood issues.

Dr. Mason understands that developing strong relationships and raising money are two important functions for a University president. He gathers a broad, diverse group of faculty and students to frame a fund-raising plan called Ten Goals for 2010. He also finds ways to show appreciation and to preserve institutional legacies. Dr. Thomas and Dr. Sayers had each been named professor emeritus at retirement. Now Dr. Mason facilitates recognition for their administrative service, and each receives the title of president emeritus.

The NCAA inquiry remains open and is time consuming. Like his predecessors who also dealt with these issues, Dr. Mason faces them continually and presses on for positive accomplishments in other areas. He clearly moves the institution forward during the interim. He lets the trustees and Dr. Portera know that although he is pleased to play a strong role as an acting president, he is not interested in becoming president. Like Dr. Wyman and Dean Bidgood, who also served as acting presidents, Dr. Mason has a long history with our institution, and he is eager to return to his earlier responsibilities.

9

Celebrating the Twenty-first Century, 2003

Robert E. Witt, 2003–present

At the beginning of 2003, trustees announce that Dr. Robert Ernest Witt will become president of the University on March 1. Dr. Witt has been president of the University of Texas at Arlington for the past eight years. He completed his undergraduate work at Bates College and received an M.B.A. from Dartmouth College and a Ph.D. from Penn State University. The trustees value the business acumen he developed during years of experience as a highly successful business school dean at the University of Texas at Austin before he became a college president.

Tuscaloosa is excited about the accomplishments of Dr. Witt and the connections of his wife, Anne. Mrs. Witt, like Mrs. Wyman and Mrs. Sayers, grew up in Tuscaloosa. She knows the campus well because both of her parents were respected members of the academic community. She knows the community well because she attended public schools in Tuscaloosa and was graduated from the University. I remember her as a classmate of Susan Rose and Paul Bryant, Jr.

Mrs. Witt went on to earn M.M. and Ph.D. degrees at the University of Texas. She taught string classes in the public schools, played cello in the Austin Symphony, and was a national leader in music education. Her son and daughter are adults and look forward to visiting the campus.

The Witts move to Tuscaloosa and live temporarily in a University-owned house while some work is completed on my third floor. Thanks to the generosity of the Warner family, the rooms on my first and second floors are beautifully furnished public rooms. The second-floor kitchen is also complete and is often occupied in preparation for University events. The Witts' first priority is to make my third floor more convenient and efficient for private family living. They are particularly interested in having a family-friendly kitchen on the third floor not only because they enjoy cooking but also because future families will be able to live more comfortably.

Chancellor Malcolm Portera with President Robert Witt and former acting president Barry Mason.

Chip Cooper, Office of University Relations

The Witts work with James E. ("Butch") Grimes, a Tuscaloosa architect, to enlarge an efficiency kitchen on the third floor into a full-sized one. The enclosed porch that held a small kitchen and laundry room now becomes the family kitchen, pantry, and laundry area. A former bedroom now connects to the kitchen, becoming a family room. The site of an original fireplace in this room is determined when the chimney is located within the wall. Mr. Grimes copies the two other fireplaces on my third floor to build a new one in the same spot as the original. He makes a new mantel that is also in the same style of the others.

Mr. Grimes owns an 1826 house in downtown Tuscaloosa with original slave-made pine cabinets. He uses the pattern and proportions of those cabinets to fabricate new ones for my third-floor kitchen.

An interior bathroom is removed, and now the northeast room on the third floor more closely resembles the original room. Workers have quite a challenge in removing old bathroom pipes. I remember the finest cast-iron pipes with lead joints being installed in the early twentieth-century renovation. Now the pipes are brittle, and patient plumbers wade through broken pipes before finally finishing the task.

The Witts use a former third-floor bedroom as a living room–dining room. Another former bedroom becomes an office for Mrs. Witt. The Witts bring their own furniture to use on the third floor so that I feel like home to them. A sleek black-and-white cat named "Bitsy" moves in with them. Bitsy likes her new home and enjoys greeting guests and being a part of events. When school groups come for tours, Bitsy is always one of the highlights.

Dr. Witt sets the pace and tone immediately for the goals he hopes to accomplish. His first priority is to fill four open vice presidencies and build his own administrative team. He tells reporters that he will focus on enrollment management while also carefully reviewing the campus master plan.

Less than two months after his arrival, Dr. Witt learns that the University's new head football coach exercised poor judgment and behaved inappropriately while on a trip. The story makes national media headlines. Dr. Witt confers with the trustees and then acts decisively. He dismisses the football coach and announces that a search for a new coach will begin right away. The University community praises Dr. Witt for creating a balanced, consistent message about the University's values. Mike Shula, a former player here, becomes the head coach.

Dr. Witt's experience with enrollment management in Texas provides a strong foundation for him now. He pushes to increase enrollment and to raise standards to recruit exceptional students through the new Honors College. My student friends, now called Capstone Men and Women, give tours to prospective students and always include me. Dr. Witt's plans for increasing the University's enrollment will allow him to admit all qualified Alabama residents while aggressively recruiting out-of-state students. The University now has recruiters who live and work in Dallas, Houston, Atlanta, and Orlando. Goals for increased enrollment are established so the University can accommodate the growth without losing its unique identity. I watch the University hum with activity and new excitement.

In June 2003 Dr. Witt presides over a special fortieth-anniversary commemoration of the desegregation of the University's student body. He welcomes forty outstanding individuals who helped "open doors" in 1963 and beyond. I find it gratifying to see Vivian Malone Jones, James Hood, Dr. John Blackburn, Wendell Hudson, Dr. David Mathews, and others, all past associates of mine, return to campus to be honored. Dr. Witt speaks to diversity as the norm now and says that the commemoration should be an "inspiration for addressing the critical issues facing our communities today." In 2005 a beautiful campus space is named Gribbin Park in honor of the Reverend R. Emmet Gribbin, one of the forty pioneers.

The University's enrollment grows, and Dr. Witt begins to plan for new residence halls. He speaks of the importance of growing the University in a balanced way, and he promotes pay increases for the faculty. The largest percentage merit raises in more than fifteen years are given.

The campus begins to show Dr. Witt's influence. He looks for areas to add benches and landscaping to provide scenic, restful places for students and faculty and to give them reason to pause and visit with one another or just drink their coffee outdoors. Campus buildings receive updates and additions. Another renovation on the Ferguson Center is completed, and an addition to the Student Recreation Center is added on its south side. The parking deck is expanded. Bryant Hall, where athletes previously lived, is transformed into the Paul W. Bryant Academic Center with the most modern technology to benefit all student athletes. A new Capstone Medical Center is completed.

To accommodate more students, Dr. Witt develops two sets of residence halls. The Lakeside Residential Community, begun in 2003, is made up of two residential buildings, a community building, and one dining hall. Riverside Residential Community has three residential buildings and one community building. We should certainly be ready for a lot of new students.

While Dr. Witt works on new initiatives, Mrs. Witt looks for ways to share her love of my history. She says she wants to take an already beautiful house and make me even more special. Of course, I like to hear that. She begins a gallery of photographs of former families who have lived with me through the years. She works with the University staff to produce a brochure and note cards that promote my history and asks the Book Arts Program in the School of Library Science to create a personalized guest book for my visitors. I do feel special.

The NCAA delivers great news in January 2004; it is closing the investigative case against our football team. Dr. Witt is relieved, and so am I.

In the summer of 2004 the Witts host a reunion of former University presidents and their families and descendants. Mrs. Witt's goal is to continue to collect stories and artifacts to make me more personal. More than one hundred relatives and descendants, representing sixteen presidents, attend from throughout the United States. I reminisce with them as they tell stories about their ancestors.

With all the entertaining, Mrs. Witt looks for ways to be more efficient. The big walk-in closet on the ground floor becomes a utility room with a washer and dryer to make cleaning party linens easier. Tablecloths can easily be stored here and accessed for outdoor events. My exterior washhouse days are long gone.

In the fall semester of 2004, the University welcomes the first freshmen to enroll in the newly created Honors College. The inaugural class has 567 freshmen, and they average in the top 5 percent nationally on the ACT test and have an average high school grade point of 3.8. The University is achieving its goal of "being a university of choice for the best and brightest."

Dr. Witt works on what he calls a series of "small actions that in the aggregate will make a difference." He calls on the campus ministries to reach out to students, and he is proactive with fraternities and sororities to encourage them to expect high standards of behavior. He looks for ways to help them keep their facilities in better shape because deferred maintenance could be a major problem in the appearance of the campus. He is focused on creating a balanced, consistent message about the University's values in every possible way.

Mrs. Witt leads a community initiative to improve music education in the public schools by adding the opportunity for children to learn to play stringed instruments. She plays with a string quartet in my music room, and she plays the beautiful Steinway piano alone. I always enjoy the lovely sounds that come from these sessions. Although Mrs. Witt moves out of the mansion in July 2005, she continues her relationship with the University as a faculty member in the School of Music.

Dr. Witt is a builder, and construction continues. Coleman Coliseum is updated. More expansion takes place in Bryant-Denny Stadium. Everywhere I look, I see new

Dr. Robert Witt talking with students.
Chip Cooper, Office of University Relations

bricks and mortar. Dr. Witt, like his predecessors, recognizes the importance of fund-raising for the University and designs his plan for the future. Goals for admission growth are being met, and the University is on schedule to be ready for more students.

I have watched almost two centuries of important events and lived with a host of distinctive, talented presidents and their families. I continue to stand and serve as a proud symbol of the University in the state of Alabama. Few, if any, buildings in the state as old as I am have been used for exactly the same purpose throughout their lives. I adapt as the times change but maintain my integrity as a historic structure. I belong to the people of Alabama, and my presence reminds them of the lofty hopes for higher education in the service of the state. I am happy to continue to be that symbol for Alabama's citizens and for their dreams of the future.

Appendix A

Presidents of the University

Alva Woods, 1831–1837 (Almira Marshall)
Basil Manly, 1837–1855 (Sarah Murray Rudulph)
Landon Cabell Garland, 1855–1865 (Louise Frances)
Short-term and acting presidents, 1865–1870
- Landon Cabell Garland, 1866, *interim*
- Arad S. Lakin, 1868
- R. D. Harper, 1868
- J. DeForest Richards, 1869, *acting*
- N. R. Chambliss, 1869–1870

William Russell Smith, 1870–1871 (Wilhelmine M. Easby)
Matthew Fontaine Maury, 1871
Nathaniel Thomas Lupton, 1871–1874 (Ella Virginia Allemong)
Carlos Greene Smith, 1874–1878 (Martha Ashe)
Josiah Gorgas, 1878–1879 (Amelia Gayle)
William Stokes Wyman, 1879–1880 (Melissa Dearing) *acting*
Burwell Boykin Lewis, 1880–1885 (Lucinda Rose Garland)
William Stokes Wyman, 1885–1886 (Melissa Dearing) *acting*
Henry DeLamar Clayton, 1886–1889 (Victoria Virginia Hunter)
William Stokes Wyman, 1889–1890 (Melissa Dearing) *acting*
Richard Channing Jones, 1890–1897 (Stella Boykin)
James Knox Powers, 1897–1901 (Lou Adeline Reynolds)
William Stokes Wyman, 1901–1902 (Melissa Dearing)
John William Abercrombie, 1902–1911 (Rose Merrill)
George Hutcheson Denny, 1911–1936 (Janie Junkin Strickler)
Richard Clarke Foster, 1937–1941 (widower—Lida)
George Hutcheson Denny, 1941–1942 (Janie Junkin Strickler)
Raymond Ross Paty, 1942–1947 (Adelaide Pund)
Ralph Adams, 1947–1948) (Frances L.) *acting*

John Morin Gallalee, 1948–1953 (Lua Caulkins)
Lee Bidgood, 1953–1953 (Emily) *acting*
Oliver Cromwell Carmichael, 1953–1956 (Mae Crabtree)
James H. Newman, 1957–1958 (Dixie) *acting*
Frank Anthony Rose, 1958–1969 (Tommye Stewart)
Forrest David Mathews, 1969–1980 (Mary Chapman)
John A. Caddell, 1975 (Lucy Harris) *acting chief executive officer*
Richard Ashley Thigpen, 1975–1977 (Mary Ann) *acting chief executive officer*
Howard B. Gundy, 1980–1981 (Janet) *acting*
Joab Langston Thomas, 1981–1988 (Marly Dukes)
Earl Roger Sayers, 1988–1989 (MarLa Stevenson) *acting*
Earl Roger Sayers, 1989–1996 (MarLa Stevenson)
Andrew Aaron Sorensen, 1996–2002 (Donna Ingemie)
Joseph Barry Mason, 2002–2003 (Linda) *acting*
Robert Ernest Witt, 2003–present

Appendix B

Chancellors of the University of Alabama System

Joseph Francis Volker, June 14, 1976–July 31, 1982
Thomas Alva Bartlett, August 1, 1982–January 31, 1989
Philip Edward Austin, August 1, 1989–September 30, 1996
Thomas Carter Meredith, June 1, 1997–December 31, 2001
Malcolm Portera, January 1, 2002–present

Denny Chimes as seen from the Mansion in the spring.
Chip Cooper, Office of University Relations